NOT A PRETTY PICTURE

The blacks will know as friends only those whites who are fighting in the ranks beside them.
And whites will be there.

C.L.R. James (1938) *The Black Jacobins*

Not A Pretty Picture

Ethnic Minority Views of Television

BOB MULLAN

Avebury

Aldershot • Brookfield USA • Hong Kong • Singapore • Sydney

Published by
Avebury
Ashgate Publishing Limited
Gower House
Croft Road
Aldershot
Hants GU11 3HR
England

Ashgate Publishing Company
Old Post Road
Brookfield
Vermont 05036
USA

British Library Cataloguing in Publication Data
Mullan, Bob
   Not a pretty picture : ethnic minority views on television
   1.Ethnic groups - Great Britain - Attitudes 2.Minorities in
   television - Great Britain - Public opinion
   I.Title
   791.4'5'08693

Library of Congress Cataloging-in-Publication Data
Library of Congress Catalog Card Number: 96-85538

PN
1992.8
.M54
M86
1996

ISBN 1 85972 498 1

Printed and bound by Athenaeum Press, Ltd.,
Gateshead, Tyne & Wear.

CONTENTS

Part One: Mass Media and Ethnic Relations

Part Two: The Survey

Part Three: The Future of Television and Ethnic Relations

LIST OF TABLES AND FIGURES

TABLES

viii

FIGURES

INTRODUCTION

In March 1958 the *Daily Mirror* reported that a number of adult viewers had vigorously complained about a new Sunday evening religious television programme aimed primarily for teenagers. The protests centred on the fact that the show, *Sunday Break,* had featured 'a coloured boy dancer'. According to the newspaper one of the letters received by ABC Television, which had made the series, was from a mother who angrily claimed that she would never allow her daughter to 'appear anywhere with a Negro'. A few years later in 1965 listeners of the BBC's *Any Questions?* were treated to similar remarks from Conservative M.P. Sir Gerald Nabarro: 'How would you feel if your daughter wanted to marry a big buck nigger with the prospect of coffee-coloured grandchildren?' By 1974, however, only a decade later, newspapers frequently carried stories of the offensiveness such racism caused to some people. For example the *Sunday Independent* reported the case of a Devon woman who accused the popular sitcom *Love Thy Neighbour* of encouraging racist taunts against her 'coloured foster-daughter'. After the programme had been broadcast the nine-year old girl had regularly been called 'Nig-Nog' and asked such questions as 'do you practise voodoo?' Evidently her young schoolmates had picked up such terms from the programme which itself frequently used them in its somewhat unfunny storylines.

Two decades later the ITC's 1995 *Programme Code* contains a specific paragraph about the use of *racial jokes*: 'Producers need to be sensitive to the possible effect of such jokes upon the racial minority concerned, as well as to changes in the public attitudes to what is and is not acceptable'.[1] It would be heartening to believe that in the late 1990s television no longer broadcast racist images, in any shape or form, but there is evidence that racism persists. For example a leading director recently claimed that British Airways disapproved of his own television commercials purely on racist grounds: 'Every time I showed them a black face or someone with dark hair or an olive complexion, they would say "too dark" or "too ethnic". They wanted to portray the face of British Airways as white with a cheesy expression'.[2] Even a channel as modern and youth-oriented as MTV does not escape such censure. For instance a number of critics of its highly successful *Unplugged* strand point out that most of the acts invited to perform on the show have been white rock'n'rollers. Indeed in early 1995 the New York City-based Black Rock Coalition held its own non-televised 'unplugged' programme, in order to showcase minority talent ignored by MTV. They argue that the racial make-up of *Unplugged* reflects a persistent double standard: 'black musicians are seen mainly as entertainers, while white musicians are more likely to be regarded as deserving of a serious showcase on *Unplugged*'.[3]

It would be quite mistaken to underestimate the strength of feeling over this issue, or its inherent complexity or importance. Consider the example of *EastEnders*, one of the soaps with an avowed social-realist and multicultural agenda. Following a series of actual attacks on shopkeepers, *EastEnders* was criticised for one of its storylines in which racist yobs attacked street trader Sanjay Kapoor and his [then estranged] wife Gita. According to one critical journalist as people mimic ideas from TV, and that since in the story those guilty of the racial attack had not been caught and punished, *EastEnders* had therefore 'sent out the wrong message'.[4]

Researchers will never be able to prove - at least to everyone's satisfaction - the precise *effects* of television on its audiences. But what cannot be denied is that television influences the minds and behaviour of individuals and cultures. For example Hartman and Husband's research in the 1970s is still salient: they attempted to discover whether or not television programmes contributed to the formation of new attitudes towards ethnic minorities, or merely reinforced existing views. Following their research they concluded that the 'indications are that people tend to notice and recall information that is consistent with their existing attitudes.'[5] It is therefore the task of any responsible broadcasting system not to allow the cultural air we breathe to be polluted by the negative stereotyping of any racial or ethnic group, and indeed to challenge such racist ideas.

This present study seeks to ascertain whether members of ethnic minorities believe television is fair to them (and others), and whether it meets their needs. It is based on the ITC's 1994 survey of public opinion which was concerned with a wide range of broadcasting-related issues, the general results of which were published by the ITC in 1995 as *Television: The Public's View 1994*. The main sample of this survey comprised a quota sample of the adult population (defined as 16 years and over) which was interviewed in-home, with quotas set in terms of age, sex and employment status, to reflect the known population profile of the adult population in the UK. The main adult sample was approximately 1,000 adults. The achieved sample was then weighted to ensure that the sex, age, social class and employment status of the analysed sample were fully representative of both national and regional populations. In addition to the main sample, two supplementary ethnic samples were drawn from representative groups of 150 Asian and 150 African-Caribbean television viewers. Quota controls were set in each case in terms of the major ethnic sub-groups (i.e. Indian, Pakistani or Bangladeshi, and African or Caribbean) and, within each of these, in terms of sex, age, tenure, working status and region, to reflect the known profiles drawn from the 1991 Census for each of these populations. The two ethnic samples, like the main sample, were then weighted in the analysis to correct any minor variations against the quota set. These interviews were conducted by interviewers from the same ethnic groups as the respondents and with the appropriate range of language skills.[6] The survey was conducted for the ITC by Paul Winstone Research, and fieldwork was carried out between 8 and 31 October 1994.

Quantified surveys of scientifically drawn samples are invaluable, but statistical data has a tendency always to remain dry and lifeless. When asked by the ITC to write up the results of this survey, therefore, the author recruited a number of focus groups, as commonly used in qualitative social research. Eight focus groups were recruited with the help of local Councils for Racial Equality. They consisted of Pakistanis (mainly Muslims), Indians and Bangladeshis, and of African-Caribbeans. The individuals who made up the groups were of a range of different ages between 16 and 60, in widely different occupations, and were from Greenwich, Kensington and Chelsea, Lambeth, and Westminster. The focus groups, all of which were moderated by the author, were recorded, and the quotations used in Part II of this volume are taken from transcripts of the discussions.

A number of people helped with information and advice: Petra Bernard (Identity TV), Debi-Bella Chaudhuri (Zee TV), Frixos Constantine, Roy Evans (MBC), June Givanni (BFI), Helen Jacobus, Sotiris Kyriacou and Lambros Lambrou, Harry Powell, Chris Myant of the Commission for Racial Equality (CRE), Gerald Winnington-Ingram (Chinese Channel), and finally Avtar Uppal and Liz Howells of the Greenwich Council for Racial Equality. I am, however, solely responsible for any of the views expressed.

Notes

1   ITC *Programme Code*, Revised edition February 1995, Section 1.4 (ii)

2   *Sunday Times*, Andrew Alderson 'BA accused of racism by director of £1m TV advert'; January 15, 1995, pp 10-11

3   Christopher John Farley (1995) 'Silence is Golden', *The Guardian,* March 31, p 11 (originally published in *Time* Magazine)

4   Harbans Singh, quoted in *The Sun*, November 29, 1994

5   Hartman and Husband (1974), p 94

6   The survey was conducted on behalf of the ITC by Paul Winstone Research and Bob Mullan

Part One

Mass Media and Ethnic Relations

1 BACKGROUND

According to the 1991 Census the total ethnic minority population of Great Britain totalled just over 3 million individuals. Nearly half of the total consisted of people of South Asian ethnic origin; indeed Indians comprised the largest individual ethnic minority group identified by the Census. The second and third largest minority groups identified were 'Black-Caribbean' people (of West Indian origin) and those of Pakistani ethnic origin.

Table 1. Ethnic group composition of Great Britain 1991

					(thousands)
Ethnic group	Great Britain	England & Wales	England	Wales	Scotland
White	51,843.9	46,907.8	44,114.6	2,793.3	4936.1
Ethnic minorities	**3,006.5**	**2,947.0**	**2,906.5**	**40.5**	**59.5**
Black	*885.4*	*880.9*	*872.4*	*8.5*	*4.4*
Black-Caribbean	499.1	499.0	496.3	2.7	0.0
Black-African	207.5	205.5	203.2	2.3	2.0
Black-Other	178.8	176.4	172.9	3.5	2.4
South Asian	*1,476.9*	*1,444.6*	*1,428.8*	*15.9*	*32.2*
Indian	840.8	830.6	823.9	6.7	10.2
Pakistani	475.8	454.5	448.8	5.8	21.2
Bangladeshi	160.3	159.5	156.1	3.4	0.8
Chinese and others	*644.3*	*621.5*	*605.4*	*16.1*	*22.9*
Chinese	157.5	147.3	142.4	4.9	10.2
Other-Asian	196.7	193.2	189.7	3.5	3.5
Other-Other	290.1	281.0	273.3	7.7	9.2
Total population	**54,860.2**	**49,861.6**	**47,026.5**	**2,835.1**	**4,998.6**

Source: Owen (1992) p. 1

It is evident that Britain is still 'overwhelmingly white'[1] in composition, with ethnic minorities accounting for a mere 5.5 per cent of the population. It is worth noting also that 'other' categories contain substantial numbers of people

- almost 500,000 in total - including the 'other-other' category, which comprises persons of mixed ethnic origin.

Again using 1991 Census statistics it is worth summarising some of the main economic similarities and differences between the white population and ethnic minorities considered as a whole.[2]

- Unemployment rates are higher for both men and women amongst ethnic minorities than for white people.

- Self-employment is more significant for ethnic minorities than for white people.

- Young people from ethnic minorities are more likely to stay in education than young white people.

- Unemployment rates are higher for 16-24 year olds in ethnic minorities than any other group in the UK.

The figures can be dissected further: Bangladeshis have the highest unemployment rates, followed by black ethnic groups and Pakistanis, while the Chinese unemployment rates are most similar to those for white people; the Chinese and South Asian minorities are far more likely to be self-employed than black people; young Black-Caribbeans are most likely to join the labour market while the Chinese are most likely to be students; the young black and Pakistani ethnic groups suffer the highest rates of unemployment.

South Asian and Black Ethnic Groups

In addition to such relative economic disadvantage South Asian and black ethnic groups are characterised by even more indices of disadvantage.[3]

- South Asian ethnic groups tend to have poorer levels of health than white people. Pakistani and Bangladeshi people suffer higher relative illness rates than Indian people. Black ethnic groups also have poorer levels of health than white people.

- The percentage of Black-African people with further and higher education qualifications is much higher than for white and other black people. However, highly-qualified Black-African people tend to fare relatively

4

badly in the labour market. Similarly amongst the highly-qualified, unemployment rates for South Asians are well above those for white people.

Despite the evidence of somewhat more positive trends - for example, the relatively high degree of home ownership amongst Indians and the size of the self-employed sector amongst South Asians - in overall terms both South Asian and black people *have higher unemployment rates than white people, across all age groups, industries and occupations.*[4]

Immigration History

In *Staying Power*, the scholarly history of black people in Britain, Peter Fryer notes that 'Black people - by whom I mean Africans and Asians and their descendants - have been living in Britain for close on 500 years'.[5] He adds that individuals of such cultures have been born in Britain since as early as the year 1505, and that in the seventeenth and eighteenth centuries thousands more black youngsters were brought to the country against their will as domestic slaves. For our purposes the most relevant historical period was shortly after World War II when large-scale immigration occurred in response to an acute labour shortage. As Fryer rightly points out, British industry 'gladly embraced' such people. In some industries the demand for labour was so great that, as Fryer puts it, 'members of the reserve army of black workers were actively recruited in their home countries'. For example in 1956 London Transport began to seek staff in Barbados and by the beginning of 1968 a total of almost 4,000 Barbadians had been recruited. Enoch Powell, at the time the Tory Health Minister, was one of many Conservatives who welcomed the West Indian nurses who had been encouraged to relocate in Britain. As Fryer succinctly describes the situation, in post-1950 Britain, 'willing black hands drove tube trains, collected bus fares, emptied hospital patients' bed-pans'.[6]

From the early 1950s onwards Britain's other 'black community' rapidly grew as rural workers from India and Pakistan also responded to official encouragement to come to Britain, and by the end of 1958 there were in total approximately 55,000 Indians and Pakistanis who had done so.

The 1948 *Nationality Act* had granted United Kingdom citizenship to all citizens of Britain's colonies as well as former colonies, and thus all these West Indian and Asian people were British citizens. In other words, their

5

British passports gave them the right to come to Britain and stay for the rest of their lives.

Despite responding to the desperate need for labour, almost invariably in lowly-paid and menial occupations, immigrants were soon made to feel most unwelcome. Fryer describes the general attitude to such immigrants evident in the late 1950s:

> Though half of Britain's white population had never even met a black person - and among those who had the acquaintance had mostly been casual - prejudice against black people was widespread ... [white people] saw them as heathens who practised head-hunting, cannibalism, infanticide, polygamy and 'black magic'. They saw them as uncivilised, backward people, inherently inferior to Europeans, living in primitive mud huts 'in the bush', wearing few clothes, eating strange foods, and suffering from unpleasant diseases. They saw them as ignorant and illiterate, speaking strange languages and lacking proper education. They believed that black men had stronger sexual urges than white men, were less inhibited, and could give greater satisfaction to their sexual partners.[7]

Since those early decades of white racism there have been many developments, some positive, others less so, but the notion of a genuinely plural society in which quite distinct ethnic groups share aspects of a common culture and a common set of institutions has yet to be realised in the Britain of 1990s in which examples of disadvantage, discrimination, prejudice, deep divisions and conflicts are still evident. Despite the widespread existence of a second generation of 'Black-British' people, Britain appears unable to rid itself of its colonial mentality.

Media and Ethnic Relations

Although individuals 'read' programmes in varied and different ways, television nonetheless has the potential to influence viewers' beliefs, and possibly their behaviour, in respect of racial and ethnic issues. It is a complex matter, but it can be argued that the media are likely to reinforce attitudes rather than create them, and there is unlikely to be any direct relationship between television viewing and the degree of racism expressed by individual viewers. This does not, however, absolve television from any responsibility for perpetuating ethnic stereotypes which may actively foster negative perceptions of black people. As Robert Stam and Ella Shohat argue, contemporary media both shape identity and also impact on communal belonging. They add that just as the media can 'exoticize and "otherize" cultures, they can also promote multicultural coalitions' and offer 'countervailing representations'.[8]

Nevertheless the media have a history of stereotyping black people, and Stam and Shohat remind us that the origins of cinema coincided with what they term the 'giddy heights of the imperial project', when Europe held sway over 'vast tracts of alien territory and hosts of subjected peoples'.[9] It is not surprising that early cinema should have adopted the popular fictions of colonialist writers such as Kipling with his stories of India, and also Rider Haggard, Edgar Wallace and Edgar Rice Burroughs who claimed to speak for Africa. In its relatively short history television too has been marked by a lingering colonial mentality through its negative imagery of black people. A number of stereotypes have been systematically created about black and Asian people: the black 'savage' who can only be 'civilised by the white man' is at least 400 years old, and the 'nigger minstrel' too has a lengthy history. This latter image implies that singing and dancing are all the black wo/man is good for.[10] Similarly, numerous Asian stereotypes which emerged out of British Colonial rule paint such people as passive and inherently docile and, paradoxically, at the same time devious with a tendency towards 'internecine carnage'.[11]

Because of their mass popularity it is the drama-serials (soaps) and sit-coms that represent the most likely opportunity for influential ethnic stereotypes, whether positive or negative.

Soaps

There are few black faces in the highly popular Antipodean soaps *Neighbours* and *Home and Away*, although they contain references to Aboriginal culture and mythology. But when in 1993 Australian-born Bruce Gyngell denounced these two soaps and claimed their popularity was evidence of continuing racial prejudice in Britain, he touched on a raw nerve and was summarily denounced by both ITV and BBC executives. The existence of such a raw nerve is itself perhaps evidence, as Chris Myant of the Commission of Racial Equality observes, that the complacency of the past has to some extent disappeared.[12] Britain's premier soap, ITV's *Coronation Street* (1960 -), has often been criticised for failing to include black and Asian characters in its avowed social-realist storylines, but although the *Street's* Salford is certainly no reflection of the actual city of Salford, as early as 1963, it did in fact feature two black characters in four episodes. Johnny Alexander, a bus conductor, was reported by Len Fairclough and subsequently given the sack; he was later reinstated but refused reinstatement on principle. Black actress Barbara Assoon also made an appearance in one episode as Johnny's wife.[13] Maybe *Coronation Street's* producers believed that issues of 'race relations' were too sensitive to be incorporated in the twice-weekly soap, but until the introduction in 1984 of factory-worker Shirley Armitage, and then in 1992 of trainee-hairdresser Fiona Middleton, black characters were seen on only rare occasions, and Asian characters, too, have been conspicuous by their absence.

In the 1970s ITV's Midlands-based soap *Crossroads* employed black and Asian actors, but many people regarded them as little more than caricatures, predictable stereotypes, such as the Asian girl in conflict with her father and the black juvenile delinquent. It was with the emergence of *EastEnders* in 1985 that a peak-time soap seriously attempted to incorporate aspects of multi-racial London into its storylines and pictures. Indeed the original cast included a considerable number of black and Asian characters, later to be both replaced and replenished. Similarly Channel 4's *Brookside* has since the 1980s included a number of characters from ethnic minorities, although with only partial success in terms of audience reaction.

If soaps are generally speaking a black-free zone, it is clear that other dramas also find it somewhat difficult to avoid what Jim Pines has termed 'tabloid race imagery'. He cites the example of LWT's peak-time fire-fighting drama *London's Burning*:

> Even a well-crafted series like *London's Burning*, for example, can't resist the final 'race relations' statement: the manner in which the noble black firefighter (Ethnic) is 'killed off' in the play on which the series was based is a story device employed in many integrationist narratives. 'Good' blacks often become integrated through some form of martyrdom![14]

Pines suggests that in both British and American police/crime dramas, black characters (and black-related situations) tend to be narrowly characterised. Quite typically villains are linked to drugs, violent street crime and prostitution, while 'heroes' are often characterised as 'noble figures' whose destiny is to 'clean up the criminalised black neighbourhoods!' As Pines acutely observes, there are few if any 'white collar black villains, corporate gangsters (à la Mafia), or computer-based defrauders in the urban crime drama'.[15]

Comedy

It is difficult to believe that LWT's *Mind Your Language* could be commissioned or broadcast in the 1990s, for this sit-com went through the whole gamut of non-British stereotypes in almost each and every episode. Set in an English language class, it consisted of a single strung-out joke: 'these-foreigners-are-hilarious-because-they-all-talk-funny-don't-they'.[16] For example Giovanni, the programme's Italian student, is portrayed as a Latin 'idiot' making thoughtless and indeed totally implausible remarks like 'Holy ravioli, these foreigners are all stupid'.[17]

The seminal *Till Death Us Do Part* (1964-74) the sit-com featuring the thoughts and attitudes of the legendary bigot Alf Garnett, raises, according to media critic Andy Medhurst, an example of the central question concerning the 'politics of comedy', namely, whether we are invited to 'laugh at him or with him'.[18] Given such features as Warren Mitchell's striking performance as Garnett, the programme's innovativeness, and the constant discussion of contemporary anxieties and prejudices, Medhurst believes that it is 'highly doubtful that its huge audience was purely composed of people laughing *at* Garnett, despite his manifest stupidities (arguing at a blood donor's session that black people's blood should only be given to other blacks, since it might turn whites into 'coons', for example)'.[19] The writer of the series Johnny Speight, also devised a comedy series *Curry and Chips* which featured Spike Milligan as a Pakistani and which was taken off air after only one season on LWT. At the time Speight commented that on ITV 'you couldn't mention black people, you almost had to treat them as if they were invisible'.[20]

Unlike *Till Death Us Do Part,* which contained no recurring black character, *Love Thy Neighbour* (1972) was itself based on a pair of squabbling neighbours, one black the other white. It appeared that the belief or premise of this highly popular series was that prejudice was to be found on both sides of the fence, and enthusiastically illustrated this by having the men of both families constantly verbally abusing each other. However, for the predominately white audience the 'resonances of "sambo" and "nig-nog" had far more weight than the corresponding "honky"'.[21] The men's wives stayed friends amidst this constant racial warfare, viewing their spouses' behaviour as merely 'silly'. Thus in this popular programme racial conflict was reduced to mere 'silliness'.

In 1976 Lenny Henry played the role of Sonny, one of Norman Beaton's screen children, in the all-black sit-com *The Fosters*. Ali Hussein believes that the show itself was a television landmark. According to Hussein it showed 'Black people grappling with their own everyday concerns, and as such, for the first time, a TV drama conceded that black people do have an independent social existence' and reality other than being mere objects of 'white hatred or compassion'.[22] Other critics (and viewers), however, saw the programme as offering little more than predictable and offensive stereotypes.

No comedy show has focused attention on the various issues surrounding ethnic representation more than the stupendously successful *Cosby Show*. Indeed famed American right-wing columnist William F. Buckley Jr., in arguing that 'race prejudice' was not on the increase in America, supported his claim by saying that: 'How does one know this? Simple, by the ratings of Bill Cosby's television show'. Buckley concluded his assertion by suggesting that 'a nation does not idolize members of a race which that nation despises'.[23] Medhurst argues that in fact the show reactivates 'all the debates about incorporation and tokenism. Are the breathtakingly bourgeois Huxtables an accurate representation of black family life? Or a model to aspire towards? Or an example of the smothering arms of white sitcom suburbia widening just a fraction to let in a family of *nice* blacks?'[24]

In obliquely answering his own question Medhurst sensibly asserts that - quite simply - one TV series centring on the life of a black family is insufficient, and that *The Cosby Show* was not designed to be the 'carrier of so much analysis and so many expectations'.[25] Unfortunately the number of programmes with black families assigned a central role is small: *Desmonds* and the *Fresh Prince of Bel Air* are two of the few.

Factual Programmes

It is perhaps worth reminding ourselves of the distinction Stuart Hall makes between 'overt' and 'inferential' racism. By overt racism he means those occasions when 'open and favourable coverage is given to arguments, positions and spokespersons who are in the business of elaborating an openly racist argument' or racist policy. Inferential racism on the other hand refers to those 'apparently naturalised representations of events and situations relating to race' which have racist premises inscribed in them 'as a set of *unquestioned assumptions*'.[26] These in turn enable racist statements to be formulated without ever bringing into awareness the racist predicates or foundations on which the statements are grounded.

Given the relative economic and social disadvantage suffered by black people, and given their exposure to relentless discrimination and racism, it is not surprising that on news and current affairs programmes black faces illustrate stories of poverty, urban crime, prisons and drug-related issues. In the absence of any explanatory commentaries, however, such visual images are at best incomplete and at worst utterly misleading. Many viewers from ethnic minorities believe their religions too are stereotyped in the media, especially television. For example Muslims feel that Islam (together with their Islamic sensibilities and community life) is depicted as an aggressive and fanatical religion, and they are critical of the way in which an issue such as the Salman Rushdie *fatwah* is reported, and how the response to it is invariably obtained from community leaders well known to hold extremist views. They also believe that there is a constant over-emphasis on certain conservative aspects of Islam such as the treatment of women, like purdah. The focus, they argue, is always on those orthodox Muslims, and not the more Westernised Muslims who nonetheless hold to the tenets of Islam. Similarly black churches, it is often argued, suffer from an image invariably characterised as one of over-zealousness and of hand-waving gospel singers.[27]

Looking back at particular moments in recent media history, Stuart Hall identifies some of the 'base-images' of this so-called 'grammar of race'. He recalls, for example, the familiar dependable yet captive *slave-figure*, the *native* and finally the variant of the *clown* or *entertainer,* and asks whether these images are as far away

> ... as we sometimes suppose from the representation of race
> which fill the screens today? These *particular* versions may
> have faded. But their *traces* are still to be observed, reworked
> in many of the modern and up-dated images.[28]

Important though it is to focus on the prevalence of media ethnic stereotypes, it is not merely a case of replacing the negative ones with more positive images. Rather it is a *range* of images that is required, produced and aimed at demonstrating the richness and diversity of black and Asian culture (including its more unsavoury and somewhat less heroic moments). Such a broader tapestry of representation would free black and Asian programmes (and their producers) from what Kobena Mercer succinctly terms the 'burden of representation'. As he expresses it, if 'every black image, event or individual is expected to be "representative", this can only simplify and homogenise the diversity of black experiences and identities'.[29]

Notes

1   Owen (1992), p 1. This statistical introduction relies heavily on Owen's analysis of 1991 Census figures.

2   This section relies on Owen (1993a), p 12

3   This section draws from Owen (1994a) and Owen (1994)

4   Owen (1994a), p 24

5   Fryer (1984), p ix

6   *Ibid* p 373

7   *Ibid* p 374

8   Stam and Shohat (1994), p 301

9   *Ibid* p 374

10   See Ross (1992), p 7. Ross adds that the stereotype implies that ' ... in contemporary society, it is in the field of entertainment to which the hopes of Black youth should orientate their aspirations: the cerebral life is clearly not appropriate for their ambitions ... '

11   Ross, *Ibid* p 8

12   Reported in Myant (1995), p 44

13   Bourne (1989), p 120

14   Pines (1989), p 68

15   *Ibid* p 67

16   Medhurst (1989), p 19

17   Anwar and Shang (1982), p 63

18   Medhurst *op cit* p 17

19   *Ibid* p 18. See also Bourden (1995), pp 29-30

20   Quoted in Kingsley and Tibballs (1989), p 111

21   Medhurst, *op cit* p 18

22   Hussein (1994) pp 134-35. Hussein adds that ' ... despite the advisory
        role entrusted to a Black social worker from the IBA to work on the
        swift development and production, it bore the hallmark of an adapted
        American formula barely sustained by the Caribbean flavour given it
        by some of the actors ...'

23   Quoted in Gray (1994), p 176

24   *Op cit* p 20

25   *Ibid* p 20

26   Hall (1995), p 20

27   See Rahi (1992), p 19. It is also worth noting that research has
        suggested that ' ... expressed interest in seeing foreign countries dealt
        with in news and current affairs is not high ...' (Wober, 1987: 1)

28   *Op cit* p 22

29   Mercer (1989), p 9

Part Two

The Survey

In Tables 2 - 58 the following notation applies:

Bold type indicates results which are statistically higher amongst either ethnic sub-group than amongst the main UK adult sample.

Italics in type indicates results which are statistically lower or less prevalent amongst either ethnic sub-group than amongst the main UK adult sample.

*   Denotes percentages of less than 0.5%.

Unless stated otherwise, Tables and Figures are based on all the respondents in each sample.

2   TELEVISION IN THE HOME

Television plays an important role in the home entertainment of ethnic minorities just as it does for the rest of the population, but they tend to possess fewer TV sets than their white counterparts. As Figure 1 shows, compared with the main sample, both Asian and African-Caribbean viewers are twice as likely to have just one set, while viewers in the main sample are three times as likely to have three or more sets.

Figure 1. Number of television sets per household

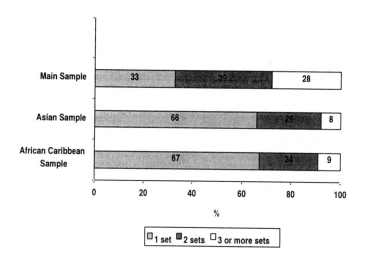

Responses to the question 'in which part(s) of the house are such sets located?' (shown in Table 2), suggest that, unlike the main sample, both Asian and African-Caribbean households tended to make bedrooms, especially their children's bedrooms, television-free zones.

Table 2. Locations of sets in household[*]

	Main Sample %	Asian Sample %	African Caribbean Sample %
Main Living Room	99	*87*	*91*
Main Bedroom	38	-	7
Child's Bedroom	18	-	-
Other Bedroom	13	*1*	-
Kitchen	10	*1*	-
Other Living Room	9	7	-
Dining Room	2	2	1
Portable	2	-	-
Other Fixed Place	1	-	-

The Asian viewers had particularly strong feelings on this issue. Many of them stressed the fact that, unlike their white counterparts, the majority of 'Indian families prefer to watch television together'. This belief in the importance of family life and the potential effect of television on it was reiterated many times by viewers:

> The family always sit together and eat, it's a time when we all get together and talk about our day, about anything, but it will all be done together...

> We switch off the telly in the evening, we may put music on, and we *talk*... if we have a problem with the children that's the time when we all discuss it...

On the question of 'television-free zones' the issue actually centred on the desire to 'protect' children from what is perceived to be unsuitable material:

> We have three TVs in the home, but not in the children's

---

[*] In this and subsequent Tables, figures appear in bold type where the number is significantly higher than would be expected, and in italic type where the number is significantly lower than would be expected. Unless stated otherwise, Tables and Figures are based on all the respondents in each Sample.

18

bedrooms; that was so that the children wouldn't go up to their
bedroom and watch what wasn't good for them ... I've heard
some Indian children do have TVs in their bedrooms, but lots
of them have it for reasons of playing Nintendo ...

Viewers in both minority samples owned a wide range of home entertainment
equipment (Table 3). The Asian viewers possessed more VCRs than either of
the other two samples, while both minority groups were lower on the
ownership of compact disc players than the main sample. Significantly, both
minorities were slightly more likely to subscribe to cable and satellite than
were viewers in the main sample.

Table 3. Household ownership of home entertainment equipment

	Main Sample %	Asian Sample %	African Caribbean Sample %
Video Recorder	83	92	75
Teletext Set	55	62	40
Compact Disc	35	15	17
Home Computer	29	34	13
Video Games	23	24	13
Satellite TV Dish	14	16	16
Video Camera	11	12	4
Nicam Digital Stereo Television Set	10	13	6
Cable TV	7	9	10
A Cable Phone	5	1	3
Video Disc Player	4	2	10
None of These	11	5	9

Apart from a slightly higher proportion of time spent watching satellite or
cable channels and Channel 4, the two minority groups watched the different
channels for similar lengths of time as did viewers in the main sample,
although Asian respondents were somewhat less frequent viewers of ITV (see
Table 4).

Table 4. Percentage share of viewing

	Main Sample %	Asian Sample %	African Caribbean Sample %
ITV including GMTV	35	29	35
BBC 1 including Breakfast TV	28	29	24
Channel 4 (S4C in Wales)	14	18	20
BBC 2	14	13	12
Satellite or cable channels	9	12	10

Compared to the main sample (26 per cent) and the African-Caribbean sample (28 per cent), almost 40 per cent (37 per cent) of the Asian sample who possessed teletext services claimed to use it every day. Table 5 itemises the services used by each sample.

Table 5. Which of the teletext services do you use most often?

	Main Sample %	Asian Sample %	African Caribbean Sample %
Ceefax on BBC 1	27	**44**	26
Ceefax on BBC 2	7	9	2
Ceefax on either BBC channel	5	3	4
Teletext on ITV	42	36	25
Teletext on CH 4	5	10	8
Teletext on either ITV/CH 4	5	2	**16**
Other Cable/Satellite teletext service	2	4	10
Use all equally	14	6	11
Depends/same channel as I'm watching	10	5	11
Don't know	1	3	4

Table 6 itemises the types of information accessed by those who possess teletext. In addition to using such services as sports information, TV programme guides and cinema listings, the most significant differences are the Asian viewers' higher use of informative or educational material. More 'educational' compared with the 2 per cent of the other two samples. Similarly Asian viewers were twice as likely to use the 'financial information' service as were the other two groups. Both the Asian sample and also the African-Caribbean sample were almost twice as likely as the white viewers to use the 'news' services on teletext (55 per cent compared to 34 per cent).

Table 6. Type of teletext information used

	Main Sample %	Asian Sample %	African Caribbean Sample %
TV Programme Guide	50	**62**	46
Sport	49	42	**65**
Weather	48	51	*31*
News	34	**55**	55
Holiday Information	29	*12*	9
Roads/travel Information	20	17	13
Regional News	12	17	13
Financial information	11	**23**	6
Local Service	11	9	*1*
Horoscopes	10	13	7
Racing	8	*1*	4
Cinemas	7	**22**	27
Games and Puzzles	7	8	5
Leisure Guide	6	7	4
Music News	4	4	6
Sub-titles	4	**11**	**12**
Children's Pages (Kids/Teens)	3	6	5
Recipes	3	4	-
Advertising	2	2	4
Computer Games	2	2	-
Consumer Advice	2	3	1
Education	2	**20**	2
Employment Pages	2	8	3
Regional Guide	2	6	1
Showbiz	2	1	-
Dating Service	1	-	-
Problem/personal Advice Pages	1	5	2

Homelife	*	1	4
Religion	*	-	2

Perhaps it is not surprising that the minority viewers, especially the Asian viewers, were more likely to claim they used teletext subtitles, and both the Asian and African-Caribbean viewers were approximately twice as likely as viewers from the main sample to do so (see Table 7).

Table 7. Usage of teletext subtitles - i.e. by calling up page 888 on the remote control

	Main Sample %	Asian Sample %	African Caribbean Sample %
Yes	25	**56**	**48**
No	75	*43*	*32*
Don't know	*	1	20

Table 8 shows the frequency of using teletext subtitles among those who have claimed to have used such subtitles at all. Almost a third (29 per cent) of the viewers from the Asian sample claimed to use such subtitling services every day compared with just over 5 per cent of viewers from the other two samples.

Table 8. Frequency of using teletext subtitles

	Main Sample %	Asian Sample %	African Caribbean Sample %
Every day	7	**29**	6
Most days	12	15	12
Occasionally	45	46	**68**
Hardly ever	36	*10*	*13*
Don't know	*	2	-

In response to the question 'why have these subtitles been used?', both minority samples were twice as likely as the main sample to say that they were used to 'counteract unwanted noise or distraction'. The African-Caribbean sample was also three times more likely than the other two samples to claim to use the subtitles in order to 'better understand' a programme viewed. But perhaps most significant is the statistic that over a quarter of the Asian sample (26 per cent) used the subtitles to 'help children learn English', compared to the low percentage of both the main and African-Caribbean samples (3 per cent and 4 per cent respectively - see Table 9).

Table 9. Reasons for use of teletext subtitles by self/others

	Main Sample %	Asian Sample %	African Caribbean Sample %
Through curiosity or for amusement	46	31	43
Because of hearing difficulties	19	15	5
To help with a language/accent	13	2	-
When there was noise/distraction	13	**28**	27
Trying to keep volume down for others	7	2	-
Because mother tongue is not English	5	14	8
Better understanding of programme	5	3	**16**
To help children learn English	3	**26**	4
To help learn to read	2	-	4
Other	1	-	-

In group discussions many Asian viewers complained about the negative stereotype that suggested that all they did in their leisure time was watch endless Hindi movies (from Bollywood), or that they listened to the music and songs from such so-called undemanding films (indeed, some of the older viewers in the Asian sample claimed that the younger generation of Asians found such films 'quite pathetic'). While ownership of VCRs in both Asian and African-Caribbean households was statistically slightly above that for the main sample, they were less likely to own more than one machine. (See Table 10.)

Table 10. Number of video recorders in household

	Main Sample (83%) %	Asian Sample (92%) %	African Caribbean Sample (75%) %
One	82	90	90
Two	15	8	7
Three	3	2	1
Four	*	-	-
More than four	*	-	-
Don't know	*	-	2

Base: All viewers with a VCR at home

Table 11 shows viewers' attitudes to videos; in their responses to a range of statements all viewers were more or less in agreement. The only real divergence concerns the statement 'I rarely get the opportunity to record the things I want to see' where both minority samples were almost twice as likely to agree with this statement than were the white viewers. This may be because individuals from minorities are perhaps more likely than white workers to be working shift-patterns and anti-social hours. In addition, many of the programmes targeted specifically at such minorities are transmitted at anti-social hours, and are therefore recorded and watched at a later date.

Table 11. Attitudes to video - Summary (definitely agree/tend to agree)

	Main Sample %	Asian Sample %	African Caribbean Sample %
The best thing about a video recorder is the control it gives over when to watch	92	83	90
Video gives me greater choice of things to watch	87	82	80

In general, watching a video is an enjoyable way for me to spend time with my family / friends	77	82	80
Having a video machine saves me the trouble and expense of going out to the cinema	70	74	70
It is often difficult for me to find the time to watch all the programmes I have taped	62	61	67
I rarely get the opportunity to record the things I want to see	36	**58**	**67**
In our house we often argue about what to record or playback	22	26	**34**

As was suggested earlier, many Asian viewers objected to the suggestion that they are preoccupied with Bollywood movies. Nonetheless such viewers do watch such films on their VCRs: as Table 12 shows, they are twice as likely as the main sample to watch such commercially recorded films more than once a week:

> If we *do* watch a lot of films it's because they're in Hindi or Punjabi ... it's the language again and for Asians over the age of 60 most of them don't speak English, so the only programmes they can relate to are those of other languages ...

Other Asian viewers added that the attractions of such films include not only the language spoken but also the music, the 'fashion and jewellery' and, most importantly, the fact that most of the films are 'made with messages and morality'.

Table 12. Frequency of viewing commercially recorded films

	Main Sample %	Asian Sample %	African Caribbean Sample %
More than once a week	11	**22**	10
Once a month	13	**28**	15
Two or three times a month	12	12	**20**

Once a month	14	14	13
Less often than once a month	11	6	11
Hardly ever/never	38	*18*	*28*
Don't know	1	1	3

Although there was heavy viewing of such movies on video by Asian viewers, viewers both from the African-Caribbean sample and also from the Asian sample had a lower rate of viewing time-shifted programming than did the main sample, as will be seen from the figures in Table 13. Indeed over one-half of the Asian sample and more than a quarter of the African-Caribbean sample claimed to 'hardly ever or never' view time-shifted programmes.

Table 13. Frequency of viewing programmes recorded earlier from TV

	Main Sample %	Asian Sample %	African Caribbean Sample %
Four or more times a week	26	*8*	*13*
Two or three times a week	32	*11*	*20*
About once a week	20	14	14
Less often than once a week	8	14	**23**
Hardly ever/never	13	**51**	**26**
Don't know	1	3	4

The general consensus among viewers from both minority samples is that, because most programmes are not specifically aimed at their interests, there is little of worth for them to record to view later:

> On the whole there are very few programmes Asians would bother to record ... so we just hire movies ... Also they don't advertise so much Asian programmes on the telly ... so you don't always know what's on.

An African-Caribbean viewer painted a picture of television as offering primarily a black-free zone:

> Most people switch the channels on, flick through the channels

and if they see a black face have a look at it and if it sounds interesting they'll watch it, or turn and turn again...it's pot luck, it's Russian roulette and nine times out of ten we end up getting the bullet in our head.

Another viewer expressed a similar sentiment and in so doing highlighted the cultural importance of television:

I don't watch a lot of TV, but if I do turn on and see a black face I say 'wow' ... that's sad isn't it ... if we had *positive* TV then our black youths would be a lot more positive about their own identity and where they're coming from.

The widely-held view amongst the African-Caribbean viewers was that they did indeed record black programmes that were broadcast, but as there were so few their time-shifting behaviour was therefore quite minimal.

Those viewers who subscribed to cable or satellite services were asked which specific channels they watched. As can be seen from Table 14, the split was generally between on the one hand the BSkyB packages and such channels as UK Gold, MTV and Discovery, and on the other hand those channels such as Zee TV and Identity which aim specifically to meet the needs and interests of minorities.

Table 14. Satellite and/or cable channels received

	Main Sample		Asian Sample	African Carib. Sample
	Satellite	Cable	Sat/Cable	Sat/Cable
	%	%	%	%
News and Information				
Sky News	95	91	90	95
QVC/The Shopping Channel	70	72	27	26
CNN International	69	**79**	59	74
Euronews	34	**72**	41	36
Parliamentary Channel	12	**71**	32	28

	Main Sample		Asian Sample	African Carib. Sample
	Satellite	Cable	Sat/Cable	Sat/Cable
	%	%	%	%
Local Cable News/Info Channel	9	**69**	22	21
Movies/film				
The Movie Channel	**79**	51	*34*	64
Sky Movies	**78**	53	*39*	69
Bravo	76	73	*24*	*31*
Sky Movies Gold	**73**	48	29	56
HVC (Home Video Channel)	18	**26**	7	21
The Adult Channel	14	15	7	13
YNT	11	14	5	7
Sport				
Eurosport	89	86	*71*	67
Sky Sports	**77**	54	*39*	74
Sky Sports Two	**59**	42	*24*	*33*
Sports Wire on Wire TV	10	**44**	22	*10*
Entertainment				
Sky One	89	86	*44*	*56*
UK Gold	87	88	*46*	*56*
UK Living	80	71	29	26
The Family Channel	**71**	61	*32*	*38*
Soap Channel	**57**	39	*24*	*31*
NBC Super Channel	11	**50**	*12*	21
Live Wire on Wire TV	10	**58**	22	*18*
Music				
MTV/Music Television	83	81	*51*	*56*
CMT Country Music TV	60	**71**	*20*	*21*
VH1 (i.e. VH ONE)	38	41	*10*	*15*
The Box	9	**56**	20	33
Performance/the Arts Channel	8	**49**	7	*10*
The Landscape Channel	7	**47**	17	18

| | Main Sample | | Asian Sample | African Carib. Sample |
| | Satellite | Cable | Sat/Cable | Sat/Cable |
	%	%	%	%
Education				
The Discovery Channel	78	84	*44*	*38*
Sky Travel	**52**	42	*12*	44
The Learning Channel	33	**59**	*12*	*26*
Travel	18	**51**	*17*	15
Children's				
Nickelodeon	**76**	65	29	*31*
The Children's Channel	75	77	*51*	44
TNT/Cartoon Network	68	74	*44*	*41*
Ethnic Minority Channels				
TV Asia	25	31	**73**	23
Asia Net	6	12	10	10
China News and Entertainment	6	5	2	**15**
The Chinese Channel	5	5	2	5
Identity (African-Caribbean)	2	9	2	**23**
Muslim Television Ahmadiyya	2	6	-	5
Namaste	2	6	12	-

Despite this, both Asian and African-Caribbean viewers expressed ambivalence about niche channels like Zee TV (ex-TV Asia) and Identity. For example a number of viewers in the African-Caribbean sample pointed to generational differences in the viewing of such channels:

> Our parents [first generation of 1950s immigrants] would cope quite well watching the normal four channels, 'cos they obviously limit themselves to what time they stay up, they're often interested in the old-fashioned entertainment. My children want the cable ... it projects a greater level of excitement and 'America' - my sons don't want to go to Jamaica, but they'll go to the States. Because the States *is in our home*.

There was also widespread concern expressed over the degree of Americanization of cable programming, especially because of what was seen as its potentially damaging influence on young and impressionable viewers:

> ... the youths run from BBC and ITV but they will sit down night and day and watch Identity TV and an everlasting stream of violent gangsta-rap videos - you know 'the bitch this, the bitch that'... that kind of thing...

A number of Asian viewers also expressed ambivalence towards niche channels such as Zee TV and Asianet which aim to cater for their needs. On the one hand they welcomed the potential of such programming, while on the other hand they expressed disappointment in what was currently broadcast. In addition, some of them were concerned about the high cost of the service: 'it's expensive, not everyone can afford it'. It was clear that for some Asian viewers it was not only imported material that they wished to watch:

> If you look at Zee TV, what is it giving us? *Bollywood*. Every other programme is a film, although they also do a bit of financial things from India and Pakistan. But they should be making community programmes *here* - informational, educational programmes. But all they want to do is entertain, just have some songs, some films ...

This theme of both the desire for - and indeed the need for -'local' television surfaced elsewhere in group discussions:

> What have Zee TV done about racial harassment? They have access to the Asian community and to the media, but have they done anything? *No*.

Despite such opinions the underlying trend indicates steady growth in the subscription to such cable and satellite channels. In response to the question 'are you interested in acquiring a satellite dish or connecting to cable TV?', those in the minority samples who were without such services were far more enthusiastic about them than were viewers in the main sample. The Asian viewers were almost twice as likely to claim they were indeed interested in such channels than those viewers from the main sample (see Figure 2).

Figure 2. Summary of interest (very/slightly in receiving satellite or cable TV)

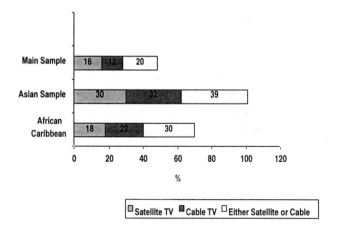

Because they consist of programmes aimed at their culture and not geared exclusively toward the white population, viewers from minority groups generally appreciate cable and satellite channels - despite some specific misgivings. The languages spoken are important, as is the simple presence of black faces on the screen. Even those viewers who express some reservations do nonetheless see the potential in cable (and satellite). As one such viewer remarked, 'cable hasn't yet got the proper resources to put on the right programmes'. Therefore the opinions expressed in Figure 3 should be of no great surprise.

Viewers from the African-Caribbean sample were almost three times as likely (55 per cent) as those from the main white sample (22 per cent), and almost twice as likely as Asian viewers (30 per cent) to agree with the statement that satellite/cable channels were *better* than the four mainstream channels of BBC 1 and 2, ITV and Channel 4.

31

Figure 3. Opinion of satellite/cable channels

Main Sample

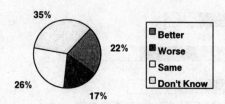

35%

22%

26%

17%

Better
Worse
Same
Don't Know

Asian Sample

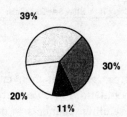

39%

30%

20%

11%

African Caribbean Sample

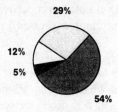

29%

12%

5%

54%

3 QUESTIONS OF IMPARTIALITY AND BIAS

No two people see the same television programme in exactly the same way: audiences take various meanings away from the same programme whether it be a comedy, an episode of a soap, or an individual news item. Indeed some critics argue that, despite the dependence of television on shared meanings, all programmes are 'polysemic', i.e. capable of bearing multiple meanings. Nonetheless from one viewer's perspective s/he may well perceive unequivocal bias or impartiality, a view which may well be shared by others too. Nonetheless, some viewers do maintain unequivocally that they perceive bias in various parts of the television output, and Table 15 represents a summary of the answers received in response to a series of questions concerning impartiality and bias.

Table 15. Impartiality of different programme types on the main four broadcast channels

	Main Sample %	Asian Sample %	African Caribbean %
News			
Fair and unbiased	69	56	41
Some favoured or discriminated against	22	29	38
Don't know	9	15	21
Current Affairs			
Fair and unbiased	65	53	36
Some favoured or discriminated against	21	23	33
Don't know	13	23	31

Drama

Fair and unbiased	71	53	34
Some favoured or discriminated against	11	11	29
Don't know	18	36	37

Entertainment

Fair and unbiased	77	66	37
Some favoured or discriminated against	8	12	31
Don't know	14	21	32

Drama Documentaries

Fair and unbiased	73	59	35
Some favoured or discriminated against	12	11	29
Don't know	15	30	37

Documentaries

Fair and unbiased	72	55	38
Some favoured or discriminated against	14	15	31
Don't know	14	31	31

Viewers in both the Asian and Africa-Caribbean samples were less likely to see any genre of programming as 'fair and unbiased' than those viewers in the main sample. Indeed across all programme types viewers from the African-Caribbean sample saw more discrimination and bias than did members of the other two groups.

Of those viewers who believed news programmes to be biased, 21 per cent of Asian viewers believed that news reporting favoured the 'British/England', while 21 per cent of African-Caribbean viewers also pointed to reporting which favoured 'whites'. Both minorities also perceived degrees of bias against 'Blacks and Ethnic Minorities' (30 per cent of the Asian viewers and 38 per cent of the African-Caribbean viewers), the Middle East and the Third World (see Table 16).

Viewers from the African-Caribbean community also believed that news programmes perpetuated stereotypes of black people by concentrating on particular issues, by providing selective images, and by not providing an explanatory context:

Table 16. Those favoured or discriminated against in news programmes on the main four broadcast channels

	Main Sample %	Asian Sample %	African Caribbean %
News	99	87	91
In favour of	38	-	7
Politics/political parties	13	10	*
British/England	2	21	2
Whites	1	7	21
Don't know	56	53	63
Against			
Blacks/ethnic minorities	4	30	38
Middle East coverage	1	17	1
Third world	1	-	15
Don't know	33	23	21

Base: All respondents saying news programmes are biased

> You know ... the woolly hat, [dread]locks, eyes-rolling,
> running from the police - in the images the police will always
> be present. It's always about crime, about violence, or about
> some rape someone's committed. Or a stabbing or loud music.

Similarly many such viewers expressed the view that the enduring and widespread image of Africa was one almost exclusively of famine or poverty. And the same viewers also complained of a lack of informed commentaries to accompany the powerful visual images:

> In Rwanda they don't talk about what the French and Belgians
> did ... they [historically] caused all this conflict.

In a similar vein many Asian viewers complained about the lack of precision and detail in the reporting of Asian issues in news bulletins:

> In racial attacks, it's not enough just to show a racial attack
> 'cos they're always showing a racial attack. They should show
> the implications of what happens to that family after there's
> been a racist attack. The family gets broken up, it's usually the
> breadwinner that's died ... they never deal with that issue.

A great number of Asian viewers, especially Pakistanis, also objected to the
news coverage of the Middle East, Asia, and, in particular, all of the Muslim
world:

> We know there is an organised attack on the Muslim world ...
> The IRA have had a campaign of bombing, and they are called
> terrorists. When there is something in the Middle East or
> concerning Muslims it is different ... look at Yugoslavia,
> everyone is Serb or Croatian, then it's *Bosnian Muslims* - why
> are they referred to by their religion?

The aforementioned viewer also objected to a specific aspect of the news
coverage of famine, and in particular how it reinforced the general coverage
of Islam:

> The [Muslim-based] Red Crescent has been at the forefront of
> relief work in Africa, but all you hear about is the Red Cross
> going in there ...

Another viewer expressed a quite different criticism of such famine coverage
seen frequently on news bulletins:

> If they show famine or any kind of natural disaster they all
> show relief from western countries, they never show the things
> that the local people do - a tremendous amount of help and
> relief is done by the local people ...

Viewers from both minority cultures, not surprisingly, tended to perceive
partial reporting and explicit bias almost everywhere on television. Indeed
bias is perceived in genres such as sports programming as well as within more
politically overt or sensitive coverage:

Cricket for instance ... if Pakistan wins anywhere in the world we won't hear about it, so you get the paper or see it on Zee TV and they show you highlights, unless it's playing against England ... if it's playing England you see it on BBC, and if it's losing you'll see it throughout the day and if it's winning you'll only get a little bit ...

Table 17 shows that other factual programming also is perceived to be somewhat partial and biased.

Table 17. Those favoured or discriminated against in current affairs programmes on the four main broadcast channels

	Main Sample %	Asian Sample %	African Caribbean %
Current Affairs			
In favour of			
Politics/Political parties	12	10	2
British/England	2	**19**	**11**
European/overseas/foreign countries	*	**14**	**9**
Whites	1	**8**	**25**
Don't know	54	38	50
Against			
Political parties	5	-	-
Blacks/Ethnic minorities	4	**39**	**41**
Minorities	3	2	-
Foreign countries/foreign people	1	5	6
Only show one point of view	4	5	-
Racial discrimination	1	8	-
Don't know	43	18	45

Base: All respondents saying current affairs are biased

As is abundantly clear from the preceding Table the viewers from both minority samples who believed such programmes were biased see them as favouring 'whites' and 'Britain/England', and indeed were ten times more likely (39 per cent of Asian viewers and 41 per cent of African-Caribbean

37

viewers) than the main white sample of viewers to believe that current affairs programmes were against blacks and ethnic minorities. A frequently expressed complaint was that 'Africa' was only portrayed in either, at one extreme, 'very interesting nature programmes', and 'at the other end of the scale is famine reporting'. There is a belief that in both current affairs programming and also single documentaries, negative stereotypes are all too frequently employed. As one black viewer put it:

> ... anything you see on these programmes is going to be things that stereotype us to be some fools, some joke, crack-addicts, Yardie gun fighting, AIDS, starvation ... everything that is related to black people is very negative. We've come to get used to that ...

Commercials also were criticised for their inaccuracy, for their implausible imagery and for their negative stereotypes. For example one viewer recalled the recent 'man from Africa' commercial:

> It's a deodorant advert ... it's so blatant, the theme is Africa but the guy must be Italian ... It's 1994, the man is a tall-dark-handsome Italian-looking man with a leopard skin cloth around his waist - he's very European, with a straight nose. Why couldn't they use an African?

Asian viewers felt that they were excluded completely from television advertising. One viewer felt the reasons behind such an exclusion were essentially political, and not strictly aesthetic:

> Why is it that banks and building societies, when they advertise on television, why aren't Asian people portrayed in them? It's almost as if we don't use banks or building societies - or we don't do the dishes at home. Why? Racism as far as I'm concerned. Probably because if one bank shows it's got lots of Asian customers lots of British people won't use that bank.

Paradoxically another viewer highlighted the fact that such a lack of representation does not make economic sense:

> Even for simple adverts like washing-up liquid or washing powder we're not seen as housewives, or as users of the

products and yet - because of our extended families - we're the
biggest shoppers going ... I know some people come out with
the excuse that 'Asian people don't go to modelling agencies',
but that's rubbish ...

**Table 18. Those favoured or discriminated against in drama programmes
on the four main broadcast channels**

	Main Sample %	Asian Sample %	African Caribbean %
Drama programmes			
In favour of			
Soaps	5	10	10
Whites	1	**24**	**31**
Politics/political parties	3	5	-
English	1	**23**	2
Don't know	72	39	52
Against			
Political parties	2	-	-
Blacks/ethnic minorities	17	**55**	**43**
Racism/racial discrimination	8	-	-
Handicapped people	5	5	-
Minorities	2	-	7
Women	2	5	2
Working class/people without	4	11	2
money	-	5	-
Too much violence/violence	-	7	-
magnified	1	4	5
Too much sex/nudity	41	16	47
They tend to stereotype			
Don't know			

Base: All respondents saying drama programmes are biased

Table 18 reports the numbers of viewers who believed that drama programmes
were biased in one way or another. Compared to the mere 1 per cent of the

main sample who believed that such programmes were biased in favour of 'whites', 24 per cent of the Asian sample and 31 per cent of the African-Caribbean sample believed they were indeed biased towards 'whites'. (Interestingly, while 23 per cent of the Asian sample also saw bias in favour of the 'English', only 2 per cent of the African-Caribbean sample did. For them it is colour itself which seems to be important.) Viewers in both minorities, however, believed that drama programmes were biased against blacks and ethnic minorities: compared to 17 per cent of the main sample who also perceived such a bias, 43 per cent of the African-Caribbean sample and 55 per cent of the Asian sample saw such dramas as being biased against their cultures.

Because soap operas play a central and strategic role in the formation of people's opinions, it was hardly surprising that it was the negative stereotyping which occurred in soaps that most concerned minority viewers. Their views on the matter were strongly held. For example, in the discussion groups there was much heated discussion of *EastEnders* and in particular the black character 'Alan Jackson' (played by Howard Anthony):

> Alan, he's typical out of sorts black male in a family structure … he's a black man with a white partner, he sensitively takes on a role (as a stepfather) which is wonderful to see … but yet still if you look at the underlying element he's almost a villain - his aggression, the physical element, he can't *talk* his way through life. That's a myth among black males. We're not all aggressive.

Another viewer talked dismissively of Alan's 'inappropriate mannerisms' and the 'things they get him to say - that boy's script is written by a white man'. As in the case of Alan Jackson and his wife/partner 'Carol', dismay was expressed at the number of mixed marriages and relationships portrayed on television:

> I think it's sad that you don't get black couples *together* … in America it's acceptable but over here you tend to have a black man with a white woman or vice versa … it happens too often for it not to be deliberate … they don't want us to be portrayed as families that have problems like everybody else but neither do they want to see us quite happy to be with each other.

In discussing both the structures and narratives of various soap operas many minority viewers believed that the 'colonial mentality' was surreptitiously at work:

> ... what it's showing is that when a black man is down or a black woman is down and we haven't got nothing at all we're all right for each other. But the moment that we step out of the 'slave plantation and start going up near Master's house' we need to have 'Master's daughter' or one of his sons by us to make us acceptable ...

'Mick Johnson', *Brookside*'s black male, was perceived as something of a lost opportunity - the character could have raised the status of black people in the serial:

> ... he's caring. But nevertheless the role doesn't show any substance. He's a pizza-parlour man ... why couldn't he be one of the real entrepreneurs in the series?

As with many African-Caribbean viewers, Asian viewers also were concerned about the negative images of Asian culture that the BBC's *EastEnders* consistently projected:

> In *EastEnders* they've shown two Asian families and in both families they show that the man is having an affair with another woman. People seeing that will think all Asian men do the same thing ... that's *not* our culture.

Another Asian viewer expressed a similar sentiment when she complained about the misrepresentation of both her culture and gender:

> In *EastEnders* when Gita chucked Sanjay out because he's having an affair with her sister, you then get the impression that he takes her out for a couple of drinks to the pub and that sorts the problem out. First of all not many Asian women go to the pub ...

ITV's *The Bill* was given credit by many minority viewers for employing a relatively high number of Asian actors. The roles they tended to play, however, were deemed to be consistently negative: 'it's always been drug-dealing, illegal immigrants, dirty restaurants ... it's never about racial harassment'. *Coronation Street*, ITV's premier soap was also chastised not so much for the misrepresentation of minority cultures, but rather for its reluctance to cast Asian characters in the first place:

> In soaps generally there are very few Asians anyway. I mean in *Coronation Street* you never see any, or *Brookside* ... yet in Manchester there are many, many Asians. And when you do have Asians it's always the same set up: we're all shopkeepers, we've all got family problems with lots and lots of interfering in-laws ...

Entertainment programmes, including comedy shows, were seen by viewers from ethnic minorities as being generally biased against blacks and ethnic minorities and conversely in favour of whites. Asian viewers (11 per cent) were ten times more likely to see them biased toward whites, while African-Caribbean viewers were thirty times (31 per cent) more likely to perceive such a bias (see Table 19). Similarly while 45 per cent of the Asian sample and 44 per cent of African-Caribbean sample saw such programmes as being biased against black/ethnic minorities, less than a quarter of that number in the main white sample expressed such a view.

Table 19. Those favoured or discriminated against in entertainment programmes on the four main broadcast channels

	Main Sample %	Asian Sample %	African Caribbean Sample %
Entertainment programmes **In favour of**			
Black/ethnic minorities	4	-	5
British	1	23	-
Whites	1	11	31
Too many soaps	1	5	-
Chat shows need improvement	2	6	5
Comedy shows need improvement	3	5	-
Working class men	-	5	-
Men	-	5	-
Don't know	74	32	54

42

Against

Ordinary people	7	4	-
Insult to people's intelligence	7	-	-
Blacks/ethnic minorities	10	**45**	**44**
Minorities	*	4	2
Politics	2	5	-
Women	-	9	2
Foreigners	1	5	-
Always same people/thing again and again	4	-	10
Only show you what they want	*	-	5
Don't know	43	40	37

Base: All respondents saying entertainment programmes are biased

Even a programme as bland and undemanding as *Family Fortunes* did not escape such censure:

> ... it's always a joke, either the contestant's name or the language. It puts you off. It's always 'the Patel' family, or jokes about 'the Corner shop'. And they take the mickey out of Chinese names, but your names are just as awkward to us, so why do that ? ...

Despite being set in the black cultural environment of South London, Channel 4's popular sit-com *Desmond's* was described by many black viewers as 'highly exaggerated', and unfortunate in that it 'spoke with such a loud voice'. A number of viewers for example argued that barbers shops were indeed important black meeting places, and were part of black culture, but that the stereotyping nonetheless spoiled the programme: 'The drama around the barber shop is pretty ok ... but there are parts of it that doesn't relate to us as black people'. Another viewer was somewhat less complimentary:

> ... there's nothing in it that's *strong*. They're speaking English lines ... short sentences ... speaking white man's words. Our barber's shop is a *real* place for black people ... people are talking about the situation in Rwanda, about Winnie Mandela ... not those jokey things in *Desmonds* ...

43

A comedy programme discussed in the discussion groups with more appreciation was *The Posse*, and also some of the sketches of *The Real McCoy*. However most discussion centred around Channel 4's *The Cosby Show,* a programme with a reputation for attracting a cross-over audience. There were two distinct views as to its precise value:

> *The Cosby Show* gives a kind of opinion that most of the black people in America live in this wonderful place, with wonderful parents taking care. Rubbish. If you go to the American communities, you'll be lucky to find a wealthy *white* family living in such glamour as those. It's fooling the young people …

Other black viewers however talked of the great potential that the programme possessed for providing positive role models and also in the raising of the aspirations of the young and impressionable:

> … it's refreshing compared to British programmes. At least you can say to your children - 'look you can be a doctor, or a lawyer, and you can be funny too'. When the son wanted to leave home, the father said, 'well you can go, but you'll have to pay rent you know'. They didn't give him the money. I can sit down with my kids and say 'this is reality'.

Unlike Bill Cosby, Britain's Lenny Henry, despite being a popular performer - certainly for mixed audiences - was nonetheless perceived to be a negative role model:

> … he's got tremendous humour, and he's even gone back to the roots [in Africa - *Comic Relief* programmes] … and it's nice that he's got a sexual connotation to things. But if he's gonna be a role model for us he's got to go the whole way - not having a black lady with him just throws it all away. It's important that people know that you are *black*, not just from the skin colour but from the other ways you behave.

Table 20. Impartiality towards selected groups of news and current affairs programmes on the four main broadcast channels

	Main Sample %			Asian Sample %			African Caribbean %		
	Fair	Pro	Anti %	Fair	Pro	Anti %	Fair	Pro	Anti %
Ethnic minorities	71	13	12	51	11	37	19	12	59
Disabled people	70	5	21	75	6	16	41	17	36
Religious groups	76	7	14	41	15	33	35	19	35
Management in industry	71	15	7	54	23	5	43	35	8
Ordinary workers/employees	74	5	17	61	9	19	47	17	25
Trade unions	62	6	27	44	11	27	36	18	34
Major services and industries	72	14	9	61	20	7	52	30	6
Health services employees	70	11	16	68	16	7	55	19	12
Education services employees	71	9	15	67	10	9	56	26	10
Social services employees	68	9	18	63	8	16	51	18	17
Govt. departments/ministries	63	22	11	52	28	7	44	37	5
Politicians	59	25	13	46	32	9	41	37	10
The police force	68	13	16	62	25	6	35	57	4
Women	77	7	12	59	20	12	41	2	24
Unemployed	66	6	25	54	10	25	29	12	51
Single parents	60	9	27	45	20	22	23	14	56

Viewers were asked whether they thought that news and current affairs programmes on the terrestrial channels were fair in the way they treated a number of particular groups, and the results are shown in Table 20. In the light of what has been seen already, the findings are somewhat predictable. For example 59 per cent of African-Caribbean viewers believed news and current affairs programmes were against ethnic minorities (compared to 12 per cent of the main white sample) and almost 60 per cent of the same group believed such programmes favoured the police (compared to 12 per cent of the main sample). More than a third of Asian viewers also believed that such programmes were against ethnic minorities, although almost half believed that such coverage was 'fair'. Similarly they were less likely than the African-Caribbean sample to perceive favouritism toward the police (25 per cent compared to 57 per cent).

Table 21 illustrates the broad similarities between all three samples in response to the question of whether coverage by terrestrial channels favours specific political parties. Perhaps the most significant statistic refers to the greater recourse to answers of 'don't know' among both the Asian and African-Caribbean samples of viewers.

Table 21. Whether terrestrial channels are regarded as favouring any political party

	Main Sample %	Asian Sample %	African Caribbean Sample %
BBC 1 **Favour any party**			
Yes	29	26	32
No	57	36	38
Don't know	14	**38**	**30**
Which party			
Conservative	22	21	28
Labour	6	5	3
Liberal Democrats	*	-	-
Others	*	-	1
BBC 2 **Favour any party**			
Yes	19	13	23
No	62	45	44
Don't know	18	**42**	**33**
Which party			
Conservative	16	11	20
Labour	3	2	2
Liberal Democrats	*	-	2
Others	*	-	-

ITV
Favour any party

Yes	14	8	**22**
No	69	48	49
Don't know	17	**44**	**30**

Which party

Conservative	5	4	**12**
Labour	7	4	9
Liberal Democrats	1	*	2
Others	*	-	4

CH4
Favour any party

Yes	9	8	**15**
No	68	47	51
Don't know	23	**45**	**34**

Which party

Conservative	2	5	4
Labour	4	2	7
Liberal Democrats	2	*	3
Others	1	1	3

Table 22. Whether non-terrestrial channels are regarded as favouring any political party

	Main Sample %	Asian Sample %	African Caribbean Sample %
Sky News			
Favour any party			
Yes	3	**13**	6
No	71	55	44
Don't know	26	32	**50**

47

Which party

Conservative	3	**13**	6
Labour	1	-	-
Liberal Democrats	-	-	-
Others	-	-	-

Other Sky Channels
Favour any party

Yes	1	**11**	2
No	68	35	36
Don't know	31	**54**	**62**

Which party

Conservative	1	**11**	2
Labour	*	3	-
Liberal Democrats	-	-	-
Others	-	-	-

CNN
Favour any party

Yes	3	4	-
No	63	43	60
Don't know	34	**53**	40

Which party

Conservative	2	4	-
Labour	-	-	-
Liberal Democrats	-	-	-
Others	*	-	-

Other Channels
Favour any party

Yes	*	-	2
No	48	30	23
Don't know	52	**70**	**75**

Which party

Conservative	*	-	2
Labour	-	-	-
Liberal Democrats	-	-	-
Others	-	-	

The question was repeated to those viewers who subscribed to satellite or cable services and were able to receive such channels as Sky News, other Sky channels and CNN (see Table 22). Again the 'don't know responses' were conspicuous, but so too was the tendency amongst a small number of Asian viewers to perceive that the Sky channels favoured the Conservative Party (three times more likely to do so than those viewers of the main sample).

Table 23. Those favoured or discriminated against on satellite or cable channels

	Main Sample %	Asian Sample %	African Caribbean %
News			
In favour of			
Political bias	13	**36**	-
Government	13	10	-
Pro American	6	-	25
Foreign countries/Europe	3	12	13
Conservatives	-	22	-
Whoever pays them/commercial bias	-	12	-
Whites	-	9	17
Don't know	65	11	31

Against

Non realistic/truthful	11	-	-
Black/ethnic minorities	6	**40**	**42**
All countries except America	8	-	**17**
Poor people/working class	-	12	7
Religion	-	24	-
Anti-establishment	1	12	-
Don't know	43	12	26

Base: All respondents saying news programmes are biased

Again when asked a question concerning any bias in the news bulletins on satellite and cable channels (see Table 23), those Asian viewers who perceived favouritism saw it mainly as operating in terms of political bias (36 per cent, compared to 13 per cent of the main sample). In addition, both the Asian and African-Caribbean samples were more likely to see such programmes as biased against blacks and ethnic minorities and as against 'all countries except America' (at least six times more likely to do so than the main sample in the case of 'blacks/ethnic minorities').

It hardly needs repeating that the evidence of this survey suggests that viewers from both Asian and African-Caribbean cultures perceive the media to be working against them, and not serving their interests. Across all genres - dramas, entertainment and factual programming - the presence of negative stereotyping, bias and partial reporting lead minority viewers to see television (especially terrestrial television) as simply representing white cultural values, and not infrequently as biased against the cultural values with which they themselves identify.

4   OFFENCE AND REGULATION

It is obvious that many black and Asian viewers will be offended by much of mainstream television, given that so much of the programming is perceived as biased and stereotyped. In addition, viewers are confronted by programmes of which they disapprove, although the programmes claim to be speaking in their voice: Channel 4's risqué *Baadass TV,* for example, is seen by some black viewers as simply reinforcing negative stereotypes of blacks as gangsters, whores and pimps, and certainly not speaking for mainstream British black culture.

Viewers were then asked a series of questions concerning offensive programming and regulation, with a first question about the degree of regulation on terrestrial channels The results reported in Table 24 paint a somewhat unclear picture of responses to this first question.

Table 24. Opinion of the degree of regulation over what is shown on the four main broadcast channels

	Main Sample %	Asian Sample %	African Caribbean Sample %
A great deal	8	7	**15**
Quite a lot	42	*34*	*22*
A little	26	26	20
None at all	3	5	5
It varies	9	14	**18**
Don't know	12	15	**20**

While the African-Caribbean sample was twice as likely as the other two samples to claim that there was 'a great deal' of regulation, all three samples settled on a figure of around 25 per cent in claiming that there was only 'a

51

little'. On the other hand, while half the members of the main sample said there was either 'a great deal' or 'quite a lot' of regulation, the equivalent figures were only 41 per cent for the Asian sample and 37 per cent for the African- Caribbeans. About half of all three groups of viewers believed that the degree of regulation on terrestrial channels was 'about right' (Table 25).

Table 25. Opinion of the current level of regulation of the four main broadcast channels

	Main Sample %	Asian Sample %	African Caribbean Sample %
Too much	12	9	14
About right	55	52	42
Too little	20	22	22
Don't know	13	17	22

When asked a question about the appropriateness or otherwise of regulation over what was shown on satellite and cable channels, over a third of those Asian viewers who subscribed to such channels believed that there was 'too little' regulation, compared to 17 per cent of both the main white and African-Caribbean samples (see Table 26).

Table 26. Opinion of the degree of regulation over what is shown on satellite and cable channels

	Main Sample %	Asian Sample %	African Caribbean Sample %
Too much	6	8	6
About right	63	32	52
Too little	17	35	17
Don't know	13	25	25
	N=638	N=241	N=34

Base: All satellite and cable viewers

Viewers were then asked if they found any programmes or other items on television 'offensive'. All three samples of viewers agreed that there were indeed, to the same extent of about 40 per cent in each case. Those viewers who replied in the affirmative were then asked on which channels it was that they had seen or heard such items. Table 27 reports that most offensive material was perceived to be on BBC 1 and ITV for all three samples of viewers. Viewers in the two minority samples were more likely to perceive offensive material on BBC 2 than were the main sample, and scored ITV slightly more highly than the main sample as an offensive channel (80 per cent as opposed to 70 per cent). Finally 16 per cent of the African-Caribbean viewers perceived material to be offensive on Sky Movie Channels compared to 7 per cent of the main sample and mere 2 per cent of the Asian sample.

Table 27. Channels on which offence is seen or heard

	Main Sample %	Asian Sample %	African Caribbean Sample %
BBC 1	68	70	66
BBC 2	49	**62**	**59**
ITV	70	**80**	**80**
C4/S4C	61	64	62
Sky Movie channel	7	2	**16**
Other cable/satellite channels	7	3	13
Don't know	4	6	5

Base: All who are personally offended by things on TV

Not surprisingly, minority ethnic viewers, when asked about the cause of offence, included 'racism'. Table 28 reports that around half of the African-Caribbean viewers who had perceived offence, and around a quarter of the corresponding Asian sample, mentioned racism as a cause of offence, compared with between only 6 and 10 per cent of the main white sample. Viewers in the Asian sample were also far more likely (especially compared to the African-Caribbean sample) to cite 'sex' as a cause of offence (61 per cent of Asian viewers cited 'sex' on ITV compared to 28 per cent of African-Caribbean viewers). Finally across the whole range of biases - political, inaccuracy in programmes and nationalism - the African-Caribbean viewers were spectacularly more likely to cite them as causes of offence. For example with respect to the charge of nationalistic bias on BBC 1, 36 per cent of the African-Caribbean viewers cited such bias as offensive compared with only 3 per cent of the main sample and 5 per cent of the Asian sample.

Table 28. Causes of offence seen or heard on the four main channels

	Main Sample				Asian Sample				African Caribbean Sample			
	BBC1	BBC2	ITV	C4	BBC1	BBC2	ITV	C4	BBC1	BBC2	ITV	C4
	%	%	%	%	%	%	%	%	%	%	%	%
Bad language	60	62	62	63	35	30	35	26	37	27	31	27
Violence	45	45	50	45	41	35	46	45	32	23	31	23
Sex	38	35	41	43	47	56	61	58	27	26	28	23
Bad example - children	20	17	20	20	14	17	24	30	28	24	35	31
Disrespect/ intrusiveness	10	10	11	11	4	7	9	7	18	20	18	16
Blasphemy/religion	7	9	8	10	11	15	12	10	6	6	7	2
Sexism	5	7	7	8	17	13	15	9	17	6	9	4
Racism	6	10	6	10	27	26	25	26	57	44	52	44
Biased/unfair progs	8	8	5	5	4	7	5	4	21	21	23	15
General bad taste	2	6	4	5	-	-	-	-	-	-	-	-
Political bias	7	5	4	5	12	14	11	11	30	13	20	10
Inaccurate progs	1	1	2	1	-	-	4	2	12	18	15	11
Nationalistic bias	3	3	2	2	5	7	6	5	36	19	19	12
Cruelty to animals	1	*	1	*	-	-	-	-	-	-	-	-
News coverage	1	1	1	2	-	-	-	-	-	-	-	-
Gays/lesbians	1	1	*	2	-	-	-	-	-	-	-	-
Others	2	3	3	4	2	2	2	2	1	-	-	-
Don't know	*	4	1	2	11	11	7	12	6	4	6	7

Base: All who are personally offended by things on TV

Although the African-Caribbean viewers considered that Channel 4 was less 'nationalistic' than BBC 1, nonetheless almost half of them (44 per cent) noted the Channel's offensive racist programmes (compared to the BBC's racist programmes which were cited by 57 per cent, and ITV 52 per cent). Channel 4's performance in particular disappointed many minority viewers:

> ... the black and ethnic minorities pay X amount of money, but the BBC put on white culture, white racist ideas. Channel 4 is no different really ... when it first started it looked like they were interested in doing something but that was soon cut short.

Respondents in each sample were asked whether they remembered in the past year watching any programmes containing an unacceptable level of violence, sex/nudity and bad language, and viewers from both minority samples recalled higher unacceptable levels on the television of 1994. For example the Asian viewers were twice as likely as those of the main sample (40 per cent compared to 22 per cent) to recall unacceptable levels of sex/nudity over the year's programmes.

Figure 4. Recalling unacceptable levels of different types of offensive material on TV in 1994

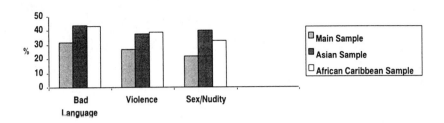

When asked whether they had switched over channels or indeed switched the TV off altogether because of sex/nudity on the screen in 1994, three-quarters of those Asian viewers and almost the same amount from the main sample who had recalled unacceptable levels of sex/nudity said that they had (74 and 77 per cent). On the other hand less than half of the corresponding African-Caribbean sample (49 per cent) said they had done so (see Table 29).

Table 29. Switching off the TV or switching over to a different channel because of sex/nudity in 1994

	Main Sample %	Asian Sample %	African Caribbean Sample %
Yes	77	74	49
No	22	17	44
Don't know	1	9	7

Base: All respondents recalling programmes containing unacceptable levels of sex/nudity

When asked the same question in relation to television violence the three sets of viewers differed widely on the issue. Over three-quarters of the Asian viewers claimed they had indeed turned to another channel or switched the set off in the face of unacceptable violence, compared to just over 42 per cent of the African-Caribbean viewers and 65 per cent of the main white sample (see Table 30).

Table 30. Switching off the TV or switching over to a different channel because of violence in 1994

	Main Sample %	Asian Sample %	African Caribbean Sample %
Yes	65	**76**	*42*
No	34	21	**52**
Don't know	1	3	7

Base: All respondents recalling programmes containing unacceptable levels of violence

Finally when the same question was asked to all those viewers who had recalled programmes containing unacceptable levels of violence and bad language, more than two-thirds of both the main sample and of the Asian viewers claimed that they had indeed changed channels or turned the set off, while only a third of African-Caribbean viewers had done so (see Table 31).

Table 31. Switching off the TV or switching over to a different channel because of bad language in 1994

	Main Sample %	Asian Sample %	African Caribbean Sample %
Yes	69	71	*33*
No	30	23	**60**

Don't know	2	6	6

Base: All respondents recalling programmes containing unacceptable levels of bad language

All viewers were asked the question 'do you feel that over the past year, television programmes have improved, got worse, or stayed about the same?' Despite the criticisms made of programmes - especially the widespread stereotyping of black people - 30 per cent of the African-Caribbean sample believed programmes had 'improved'. However the predominant view of all three samples of viewers was that programmes had 'stayed about the same': 59 per cent each for the main and Asian samples, and 42 per cent of the African-Caribbean viewers (see Figure 5).

Figure 5.   Opinion of TV programmes over the past year

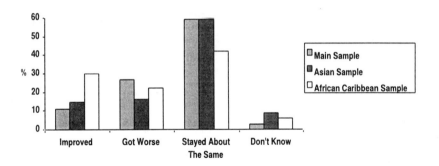

A similar question was asked of all viewers in respect of the improvement or otherwise of individual channels in 1994. Again, and perhaps no great surprise, all three sets of viewers tended to argue that channels, terrestrial and cable/satellite, had 'stayed about the same'. It is in fact a difficult question to answer, especially in respect of a channel's performance over a year. Interestingly enough - again given the criticism of specific programmes reported earlier - the African-Caribbean viewers were more likely than the other two groups to see improvement in all channels. For example in respect of ITV, viewers from *both* the Asian sample (20 per cent) and African Caribbean sample (35 per cent) were more likely to cite improvement than the main sample (12 per cent). African-Caribbean viewers who subscribed to either satellite or cable services tended to see more improvement in satellite channels (29 per cent) and cable channels (45 per cent) than either of the other two groups (17 per cent and 12 per cent of the main sample, and 18 and 12 per cent of the Asian sample: Table 32).

Table 32. Opinion of channels over the past year

	Main Sample %	Asian Sample %	African Caribbean Sample %
BBC 1			
Improved	10	16	28
Got worse	23	9	21
Stayed about the same	62	67	45
Don't know	4	8	6
BBC 2			
Improved	10	12	23
Got worse	14	9	14
Stayed about the same	67	66	54
Don't know	10	12	10
ITV			
Improved	12	20	35
Got worse	23	12	14
Stayed about the same	60	58	45
Don't know	4	9	6
C4/S4C			
Improved	12	16	36
Got worse	15	11	7
Stayed about the same	62	58	45
Don't know	10	16	12

	Main Sample 624 %	Asian Sample 39 %	African Caribbean Sample 34 %
Satellite Viewers:			
BSkyB and other satellite channels			
Improved	17	18	**29**
Got worse	6	5	2
Stayed about the same	54	47	47
Don't know	22	**30**	23

	Main Sample 287 %	Asian Sample 16 %	African Caribbean Sample 14 %
Cable Viewers:			
Cable			
Improved	12	12	**45**
Got worse	7	5	5
Stayed about the same	51	*34*	*30*
Don't know	30	**50**	20

Children and Television

All viewers were asked the question 'would you say it is mainly the responsibility of parents or of broadcasters to make sure that children don't see unsuitable programmes?' Figure 6 presents the findings. Viewers from the main sample (64 per cent) were much more likely than viewers from the Asian sample (32 per cent) and the African-Caribbean sample (43 per cent) to see the responsibility as belonging mainly to the parents. Conversely viewers from the Asian sample (28 per cent) and the African-Caribbean sample (12 per cent) were much more likely than those from the main sample (6 per cent) to see such responsibility as lying mainly with the broadcasters. A substantial proportion of viewers from the two minority samples saw the responsibility as one equally shared by both broadcasters and parents: Asian viewers 37 per cent, and African-Caribbean viewers 44 per, compared to 29 per cent of the main sample.

Figure 6.   Where responsibility lies for protecting children from unsuitable programmes

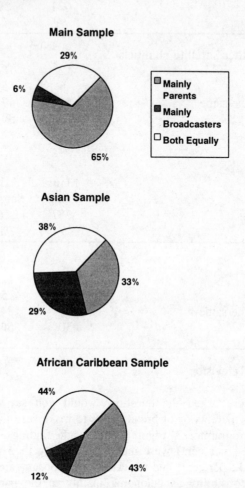

More than three-quarters of all three samples of viewers were aware of the idea of the 'watershed' for the main terrestrial channels of BBC 1, BBC 2, ITV and Channel 4 (S4C), although viewers from ethnic minorities were slightly less likely to be aware of the watershed than were those from the main sample (16 and 15 per cent as opposed to 9 per cent: Table 33).

Table 33. Awareness of watershed for BBC 1, BBC 2, ITV and CH4 (in Wales S4C)

	Main Sample %	Asian Sample %	African Caribbean Sample %
Yes	87	75	77
No	9	16	15
Don't know	4	9	9

When questioned further about the precise timings of the 'watershed', it was evident that not all viewers who claimed they knew of the policy were aware that it was set at 9.00 pm. As the findings in Table 34 show, over three-quarters of all viewers correctly identified the time as 9.00 pm. However both the Asian viewers and African-Caribbean viewers were three times more likely than viewers from the main sample to believe that the watershed was later than 9.00 pm, and this belief was expressed in connection with all four channels.

Table 34. Do you know what time the watershed is for BBC 1, BBC 2, ITV and CH4 (in Wales S4C)?

	Main Sample	Asian Sample	African Caribbean Sample
BBC 1	%	%	%
Earlier than 9.00 pm	8	10	16
9.00 pm	80	61	55
Later than 9.00 pm	7	20	21
Don't know	6	8	8
BBC 2	%	%	%
Earlier than 9.00 pm	8	8	15
9.00 pm	78	64	56
Later than 9.00 pm	4	16	19

61

Don't know	8	11	9
ITV	%	%	%
Earlier than 9.00 pm	8	7	11
9.00 pm	79	62	59
Later than 9.00 pm	7	**23**	**21**
Don't know	6	8	8
C4/S4C	%	%	%
Earlier than 9.00 pm	8	8	10
9.00 pm	77	63	56
Later than 9.00 pm	7	**19**	**21**
Don't know	9	10	12

Base: All respondents aware of watershed

When asked whether they thought the 9.00 pm watershed was set at the correct time all three samples of viewers were generally in agreement. Almost three quarters of *all* viewers believed it to be 'about right' while between a fifth and a quarter considered 9.00 pm to be 'too early'. Only a tiny proportion believed the time was 'too late' (see Table 35).

Table 35. Opinion of 9.00 pm watershed time for ITV, Channel 4 and the BBC

	Main Sample %	Asian Sample %	African Caribbean Sample %
Too early	21	18	25
Too late	5	3	2
About right	70	72	69
Don't know	4	7	4

Many Asian viewers believed that there is, in fact, little for them actually to do, in terms of the protection of their children from screen images of sex/nudity, violence and bad language:

We don't have to tell them not to watch it. As a child, if a
rude scene came on you left the room discreetly, you didn't
have to be monitored, your parents didn't have to tell you to
leave the room ... a lot of it is self-monitoring in our culture.
You just don't watch rude scenes in mixed-company.

There was, nonetheless, support for the view that the watershed was too early:

Nine o'clock is too early. Many children don't go to bed 'till
later. Besides there's lots of violence and rude scenes before
then.

All viewers were then asked whether they knew that a number of satellite and
cable channels had two watershed times, one set at 8.00 pm for '15' rated
films, and the other at 10 pm for '18' rated films. All three samples of
viewers tended to be either unaware, or simply said they didn't know. Only
about 10 per cent of viewers in each group were actually aware that there was
indeed a twin watershed for such channels (see Table 36).

**Table 36. Awareness of the twin 8.00 pm and 10.00 pm watershed times
for some satellite/cable channels**

	Main Sample %	Asian Sample %	African Caribbean Sample %
Yes, aware	14	11	15
No, not aware	69	43	47
Don't know	18	46	38

Again there was a high proportion of 'don't knows' - especially among the
minority viewers - when they were asked their opinions of the dual watershed
of some satellite and cable channels. Viewers from the main sample were
more likely to believe that both times were 'about right' (58 per cent)
compared with those of the Asian sample (30 per cent) and also the African-
Caribbean sample (40 per cent). Regarding the early time of 8.00 pm for '15'
rated films, almost a third of the Asian viewers (28 per cent) believed this to
be 'too early', compared with 20 per cent of the main sample and 19 per cent
of the African-Caribbean sample (see Table 37).

Table 37. Opinion of the 8.00 pm and 10.00 pm watershed times for some satellite/cable channels

	Main Sample %	Asian Sample %	African Caribbean Sample %
8 o'clock too early	20	**28**	19
8 o'clock too late	2	-	1
10 o'clock too late	5	7	4
10 o'clock too late	3	3	3
Prefer 9 o'clock	9	10	5
Both times about right	58	*30*	*40*
Don't know	13	**36**	**35**

Perhaps the reason for this was that Asian viewers were slightly more aware that there were parental control devices on a number of satellite and cable services (see Table 38).

Table 38. Awareness of parental control devices on some satellite and cable services

	Main Sample %	Asian Sample %	African Caribbean Sample %
Yes, aware	24	28	18
No, not aware	67	*33*	*49*
Don't know	18	**39**	**34**

Viewers from ethnic minorities appear to be especially concerned over the way in which television programmes make the job of transmitting their own culture to their children even more difficult than it already is. One viewer succinctly expresses such a concern:

> ... my children get from telly programmes that perhaps there
> is no transport system in Pakistan. Or they'll just show

extreme poverty, famine, or flood. So the Indian, Bangladeshi or Pakistani children who are British-born are cut off from their country.

Another viewer expressed her concern in a much more personal manner:

> Our children who are born here seem to imagine that their countries are, you know - there's no roads, no transport, just mud huts. When you show them your photographs and you want to take them, they say 'oh no I'm not going - I'll get malaria, or typhoid' ...,

while another viewer observes the conflicts that their children have to endure because of the conflicting messages they receive on the one hand from their parents and on the other hand from popular television programmes:

> It's difficult enough for parents to teach them their culture in this country anyway, but that's being contradicted in the evenings when they see *soaps* and other totally westernised programmes that have no bearing on their culture at all. So the children are being caught in sort of very difficult situations ... what do you tell the children? It's always the negative thing - an Asian girl going off with a boy. Do we tell them it's right or wrong? We tell them it's wrong, but on the media it shows such things as being 'independent', something they have to do ...[1]

Amongst the African-Caribbean sample of viewers too, there was concern over the representation of black culture on television. In particular there was anxiety that black young people's cultural identities were under threat from the predominance of white programming:

> I don't want my children to watch white television. It's not going to stimulate them ... when you see stereotyped programming, they influence children. You find black children leaving black homes - they don't want to be black ... I don't think there's nothing on television that represents their culture, or it's on after 11.00 at night ... at Christmas Eve there was a nice thing from Jamaica about Reggae music [Channel 4], but it came on at midnight and it was presented by a white person.

Let *us* have some credit for doing something ...

One of the few programmes cited by black viewers as having a relatively *positive* influence on children was the American-produced Channel 4 educational show *Sesame Street*. In particular both its on-screen 'egalitarianism' and associated absence of stereotyping greatly appealed to such viewers:

> The only programme I let my children watch is *Sesame Street* ... they have Spanish, black children ... they're all equal. No one is superior. On *Playbus* a black man comes on with a yellow tie, flowery shirt, red trousers and he'll be acting the fool. It's terrible.

The same viewer recalled how radically different it was for her as a child in the sixties when her father believed it was important for her to embrace British culture, despite its inherent racism:

> Our parents [first generation immigrants] didn't allow us to ever sit and watch racist programmes on our own. My dad didn't say 'You mustn't watch it', 'cos he felt that if you're in England you need to understand English people...

Table 39. Attitudes to children and television - Summary (definitely agree/tend to agree)

	Main Sample %	Asian Sample %	African Caribbean Sample %
Parents should encourage their children to watch TV in limited amounts	89	87	88
Parents should discourage their children from watching too much TV	88	86	85
Parents should discuss their children's choice of what to watch on TV with them	88	88	83

Parents should discuss what children have seen on TV with them	87	85	85
Parents should influence **what types of programmes** their children watch by example	87	81	81
Parents should influence **how much** TV their children watch by example	86	*77*	81
Parents should restrict the total amount of time that children can watch TV	84	80	81
Parents should forbid their children from watching certain programmes altogether	83	86	79
Parents should gradually relax the control they exert over their children's TV viewing as the children grow older	80	*68*	77
Parents should try to watch TV with their children as much as possible	79	*66*	72
Parents should set special hours when their children can watch TV	74	**88**	77
Parents can't reasonably be expected to keep an eye on their children's TV viewing all the time	65	**78**	**80**
Parents should encourage their children to watch TV	39	*29*	**52**
Parents should allow their children the freedom to watch whatever they like on TV	13	13	**23**

Table 39 presents a summary of the viewers' attitudes toward the relationship between children and television. On the majority of statements listed, all three samples of viewers tend to be in agreement. Where the three groups of viewers do differ it is generally over the Asian sample's cautious view that children need to be protected from any possible unwanted programming. For example in response to the statement 'parents should set special hours when their children can watch TV', 88 per cent of the Asian sample concurred, compared with 74 per cent of the main sample and 77 per cent of the African-Caribbean sample.

Notes

1   See Gillespie (1993). Her analysis of 'soap viewing' amongst Punjabi youth in Southall points to such conflicts (1993: 26):

' ... It proposed that viewing can be an antagonistic ritual because parents' and young people's value judgments - in real life, and about screen life - differ. Thus viewing is a playfully combative experience, characterised by both intimacy and censure. It can lead to intimate talk, especially with mothers, and it can also allow young people to challenge parental values. However, it often results in censorious talk on the part of parents as they seek to guide and discipline their children and to exploit the situation for didactic purposes ...'

5   THE IMPORTANCE OF TELEVISION

The central and currently unmovable element of the schedule of mainstream television channels is the news, and individuals say they rely primarily on television news for information of events going on in the world around them. Table 40 reports the various sources of news that viewers from all three samples use, with the columns showing the source the viewer mentioned first and then all additional sources.

Table 40. Sources of news

Mentioned	Main Sample		Asian Sample		African Caribbean Sample	
	1st %	Other %	1st %	Other %	1st %	Other %
Television	72	96	71	94	74	96
Any newspaper	15	77	9	70	11	71
Radio	10	57	14	66	12	59
Teletext	1	5	2	9	2	8
Talking to people	1	18	3	29	1	20
Magazines	*	2	-	3	-	9
None	-	-	-	2	-	7
Don't know	*	*	2	2	-	-

It is evident that generally speaking viewers from all three samples rely primarily on television as the main source for news. In addition, viewers from the Asian sample were more likely than the other two samples to mention radio and 'talking to people' as additional sources of news.

The findings reported in Table 41 demonstrate that the Asian sample was again more likely to mention radio as an additional source of local news (almost equally with television), as well as 'talking to people' as such a source. All three samples of viewers equally cited newspapers and television as the first source of news about their local area.

Table 41. Sources of news about local area

Mentioned	Main Sample 1st %	Main Sample Other %	Asian Sample 1st %	Asian Sample Other %	African Caribbean Sample 1st %	African Caribbean Sample Other %
Any newspaper	42	80	35	73	33	69
Television	36	65	26	57	38	69
Radio	12	46	23	60	13	51
Talking to people	9	35	15	54	12	41
Magazines	*	2	-	4	3	6
Teletext	*	3	1	6	1	1
Newsletters	-	*	-	*	*	1
Advertising/posters/ Shop window	-	*	-	1	-	1
Other	*	*	-	1	-	1
None	-	-	-	2	-	9
Don't know	1	1	1	1	-	-

Similar findings were reported with respect to the source of news about the 'whole of the UK'. This time it was the African-Caribbean sample (18 per cent) as well as the Asian sample (16 per cent) that were much more likely to cite radio as a source of news compared to the main sample (9 per cent). Television remained the major source for all three sets of viewers (almost two-thirds of each sample: Table 42).

Table 42. Source of most news about the whole of the UK

	Main Sample %	Asian Sample %	African Caribbean Sample %
Television	66	65	70

Any newspaper	14	13	17
Radio	9	**16**	**18**
Talking to people	3	4	2
Magazines	1	-	1
Teletext	1	2	1
None	2	-	-
Don't know	6	3	3

For news about 'Europe and the rest of the world' there was general similarity in choice of medium. Again television was the major source of such news with 75 per cent of the main sample citing it, compared to 66 per cent of the African-Caribbean sample and 63 per cent of the Asian sample. The Asian sample continued to 'talk to other people' about 'Europe and the rest of the world' (6 per cent), which is hardly surprising given the wide variety of languages spoken among the Asian communities (see Table 43).

Table 43. Source of most news about Europe and the rest of the world

	Main Sample %	Asian Sample %	African Caribbean Sample %
Television	75	63	66
Any newspaper	15	16	15
Radio	8	7	14
Teletext	2	3	3
Magazines	*	-	4
Talking to people	-	6	3
Other	*	1	-
None	1	-	*
Don't know	2	5	6

Earlier, in Chapter 3, we saw that minority viewers did not judge factual programmes (including news) on television to be especially fair or unbiased. Such programmes were considered to be negative (with a concentration on such items and images as poverty and famine), anti-black, anti-Muslim and generally biased against ethnic minorities. It is therefore hardly surprising that in response to the question 'which do you generally trust to present the most fair and unbiased news coverage?' the viewers from the Asian and African-Caribbean samples were less enthusiastic about television than the main sample. Whereas 71 per cent of the main white sample cited television as 'most fair and unbiased', only 51 per cent of the African-Caribbean and 54 per cent of the Asian samples agreed. The African-Caribbean sample were more likely (20 per cent) to cite radio as 'most fair and unbiased' than the main sample (12 per cent) or indeed the Asian sample (13 per cent). The findings, presented in Table 44, demonstrate that very few replied 'none' to the question.

Table 44. Source of most fair and unbiased national and international news

	Main Sample %	Asian Sample %	African Caribbean Sample %
Television	71	54	51
Radio	12	13	20
Newspapers	7	13	9
Teletext	3	2	5
Magazines	1	4	2
None	1	4	7
Don't know	6	11	7

A related question asked viewers their opinions as to whence they derived the 'clearest understanding' of such national and international news. The Asian sample (17 per cent) were twice as likely as the main sample (7 per cent) and much more likely than the African-Caribbean sample (10 per cent) to cite newspapers, although television was the source most cited by all three samples (see Table 45).

Viewers in the Asian sample were much less likely (35 per cent) than both the main and African-Caribbean samples of viewers (55 per cent each) to cite television as the source of the 'most fair and unbiased local and regional news' (see Table 46). Conversely the Asian sample were more likely (24 per cent) than the main sample (15 per cent) or the African-Caribbean sample (18 per cent) to cite radio as the most 'fair or unbiased source'. The Asian viewers were also more likely to favour newspapers than were the other two samples of viewers.

Table 45. Source offering the clearest understanding of national and international news

	Main Sample %	Asian Sample %	African Caribbean Sample %
Television	78	*63*	73
Radio	9	9	11
Newspapers	7	**17**	10
Teletext	3	3	5
Magazines	*	2	1
Talking to people	-	-	1
None	*	1	1
Don't know	3	8	3

Table 46. Source of the most fair and unbiased local and regional news

	Main Sample %	Asian Sample %	African Caribbean Sample %
Television	55	*35*	55
Newspapers	21	25	15
Radio	15	**24**	18
Magazines	1	1	*
Teletext	1	1	1
Talking to people	*	-	1
None	1	4	4
Don't know	6	11	4

Attitudes To Television

Many Asian viewers admitted, albeit reluctantly, they were somewhat heavy viewers of television. Despite their avowed disinterest, and indeed at times disapproval, of much of the available programming, such viewers nonetheless spent considerable hours in front of the screen. One viewer gave a cultural reason for such amounts of viewing:

> I think it's very difficult for Asian people ... the Indian man might go to the pub, the Indian woman wouldn't go to the pub ... some Muslims might go to the pub ... So really there's no alternative but to stay at home [and watch the television] ... but a lot of people go to the religious places just for the sake of cultural reasons and for social reasons ... not just for prayers ...

Another Asian viewer added that in her opinion there was 'no alternative but to simply watch a Hindi film'. In addition a number of Asian viewers complained about the scheduling of programmes designed primarily for their consumption:

> ... you'll see Asian programmes mainly in the morning, and at off-peak times ... In peak times there's nothing. They think the Asian community just wants to watch films, that they have no culture. If you're going to positively promote any programming for the ethnic communities it has to be at peak times, or near peak times.

Even if viewers reluctantly turned to BBC2's Saturday morning Asian programmes - if they were not busily working - they were still far from satisfied with what they saw:

> Even on Saturdays when they show *Chanakya* [47 episodes about Vishnu Gupta] this is only targeted to one group in the Asian community. Not *all* the different religions.

The issue of religious programming surfaced in many of the conversations of the discussion groups. For example a viewer from the Black-Caribbean community angrily noted that 'recently on television there was a choir competition ... all white, no black choirs', while an Asian viewer assumed that it was unlikely that there would be any more religious programmes broadcast on the main terrestrial channels, especially those concerning

74

religions of her culture:

> White people get quite a lot of religious coverage anyway so they're not likely to ask for more. But there's nothing on TV that regularly covers Indian festivals. For Asians their culture and religion are so *interwoven* ...

Table 47. Strength of interest ('very interested' or 'quite interested') in different programme types

	Main Sample %	Asian Sample %	African Caribbean Sample %
National news	91	91	95
Local and regional news	89	85	92
Films - recent releases	88	72	81
International news	81	89	**92**
Adventure or police series	80	55	63
Nature and wildlife programmes	80	64	67
Drama documentaries	75	55	76
Plays and drama serials	73	49	69
Situation comedy shows	71	60	72
Soap operas	66	57	74
Older or classic cinema films	65	48	57
Quiz or panel games shows	65	58	70
Health & medical programmes	64	70	**85**
Holiday & travel programmes	64	41	48
Current affairs programmes	61	54	**70**
Hobbies & leisure programmes	60	42	54
Sports programmes	58	58	66
Variety shows	58	52	66
Alternative comedy shows	57	62	**74**
Chat shows	56	50	**70**
Films suitable only for adults	53	37	**70**
Progs from/about european countries	50	35	54
Consumer affairs	49	36	53
Education programmes for adults	49	**60**	77
Women's programmes	45	50	**61**
Science programmes	44	**54**	**59**

Pop or rock music	41	*28*	44
Programmes about politics	32	38	**44**
Arts programmes	29	23	33
Programmes for older children	28	**40**	**41**
Business & financial programmes	26	33	38
Church services	23	*6*	**63**
Programmes for use in schools	21	**38**	**56**
Programmes for the under 5's	20	**33**	**35**
Programmes about religion	19	**53**	**65**

Table 47 shows how viewers responded when asked 'how interested' they were in a number of different types of programmes. Asian viewers were less likely to be as interested as the other two samples in such genres as wildlife, drama-docs, 'adventure or police series', plays and drama serials, sitcoms, old movies, holiday programmes, adult-movies, pop music and church services. African-Caribbean viewers appeared keen to receive 'health and medical' programming, 'alternative comedy' shows, chat shows, women's programmes, adult movies and, especially, church services. Most significantly viewers from both minority samples were far more likely than those from the main sample to request more programmes for use in schools, programmes for the under 5s and programmes about religion. In this last category 65 per cent of the African-Caribbean sample expressed interest in programmes about religion as did 53 per cent of the Asian sample, compared with only 19 per cent of the main white sample.

Table 48. How viewers decide what they are going to watch on television (often/occasionally)

	Main Sample %	Asian Sample %	African Caribbean Sample %
I watch the same programmes because I like them and know when they are on	93	*77*	91
I read the TV listings that appear in the newspaper	75	*58*	71

I make selections from TV Times, Radio Times or some other TV listings magazines	71	*47*	63
I choose on the basis of advance programme trailers shown on TV	70	*53*	*55*
I watch programmes picked by other family members or people in my house	65	63	*50*
I follow recommendations of friends	61	56	48
I skip from channel to channel until I find something interesting	59	60	**71**
I watch one programme and then leave the set tuned to the same channel	43	*29*	49
I plan what to watch several days in advance	43	*26*	44

When asked for their reactions to statements about their viewing choices, the majority of viewers from all samples already tended to know what was available or relied on specialist listings magazines or newspaper columns. On the other hand, 71 per cent of the African-Caribbean sample said that often or at least occasionally they channel-hopped in search of 'something interesting' to watch, compared to 60 per cent of the Asian sample and 59 per cent of the main sample. Overall Asian viewers appeared to be more discriminating in what they watched and for example were reluctant (only 29 per cent) to watch a specific programme and then leave the set tuned to the same channel (compared to 49 per cent of the African-Caribbean viewers and 43 per cent of the main sample: Table 48).

Table 49 highlights how television generally fits into the lives of those viewers from the Asian and African-Caribbean communities. Compared to only 19 per cent of the main sample who stated that they didn't 'have a chance to see enough' television, 36 per cent of the Asian sample and 44 per cent of the African-Caribbean sample expressed the same opinion. Conversely they were less likely than the main sample (47 per cent) to say that they spent 'too much time watching television' (10 per cent of Asian and 11 per cent of African-Caribbean viewers).

Table 49. Opinion of amount of time spent watching television

	Main Sample %	Asian Sample %	African Caribbean Sample %
Watch the right amount	60	*47*	*41*
Spend too much time watching TV	19	*10*	*11*
Don't have a chance to see enough	19	**36**	**44**
Other answers	1	4	1
Don't know	2	4	3

All the viewers were then asked to specify precisely why they watched television (Table 50). Once again viewers from the Asian sample were less likely than viewers from the other two samples to provide passive reasons. For example only 22 per cent said they watched 'as an escape from everyday concerns' compared to 34 per cent of the African-Caribbean sample and 40 per cent of the main sample. Most significantly viewers from both minority samples were less likely to say that they watched TV because they simply felt like watching TV: whereas 93 per cent of the main sample stated that they did so, only 54 per cent of the Asian sample and 61 per cent of the African-Caribbean did so. The African-Caribbean sample were more likely to look for educational benefits ('I watch because I think I can learn something') and also so that they could subsequently be sociable ('I watch a programme because everyone I know is watching and will be talking about it afterwards').

Table 50. Reasons for watching television

	Main Sample %	Asian Sample %	African Caribbean Sample %
I watch to see a specific programme I enjoy very much	95	*87*	91
I watch just because I feel like watching TV	93	*54*	*61*

I watch to see a special programme that I have heard a lot about	90	*72*	*82*
I watch just because it is a pleasant way to spend an evening	73	*54*	66
I watch because I think I can learn something	67	61	**76**
I start watching because someone else is watching and seems to be interested	53	*37*	45
I start on one programme and then I find myself watching for the rest of the evening	49	*31*	50
I watch because there is nothing better to do at the time	48	47	56
I watch to be sociable when others are watching	45	*36*	45
I turn on the set just for company	41	42	44
I watch as an escape from everyday concerns	40	*22*	34
I watch in case I'm missing something good	40	41	**68**
I watch just for 'background' whilst I'm doing something else	38	36	44
I watch a programme because everyone I know is watching and will be talking about it afterwards	31	30	**48**
I keep watching to put off doing something else I should do	29	*17*	27
I watch to ignore or get away from people around me	16	19	20

Viewers in the three samples were then given a further series of statements about their general attitudes to television with which they could either agree or disagree, and the results are shown in Table 51. Among the most interesting findings were that 71 per cent of the main sample agreed with the statement that 'the four main broadcast channels give me all the viewing choices I want', compared with only 56 per cent of the Asian sample and 35 per cent of the African-Caribbean sample. Concomitantly, viewers from the African-Caribbean sample were more likely to agree with the statement that 'satellite or cable offers a far wider choice of programmes' than were the other sets of viewers (73 per cent compared to 62 per cent of the main sample and 63 per cent of the Asian sample).

Over 60 per cent of both the Asian and African-Caribbean samples compared to 38 per cent of the main sample believed that 'things that are likely to upset people should never be shown on television'. Minority viewers also appear to be more likely to be channel hoppers: for example 55 per cent of the African-Caribbean viewers compared to 25 per cent of the main sample agreed that they 'switched from channel to channel to try to follow more than one programme at a time'.

Not surprisingly only 45 per cent of the Asian sample compared with 61 per cent of the main sample and 67 per cent of the African-Caribbean sample believed that viewers should be free to pay for 'violent or pornographic' programmes not available on existing channels.

Table 51. Broad attitudes to television - Summary (definitely agree/tend to agree)

	Main Sample %	Asian Sample %	African Caribbean Sample %
I can always find plenty of other things to do if there is nothing I want to watch on TV	92	80	84
It's up to me what I choose to watch on TV - not the regulators	83	65	75
The four main broadcast channels give me all the viewing choices I want	71	56	35

I dislike the way films are sometimes cut even when they are broadcast after 10.00 pm	71	*62*	78
Satellite or cable offers you a far wider choice of programmes	62	63	**73**
Pay channels should have exactly the same restrictions on what they are allowed to show as other TV channels	62	57	*42*
If people want to pay extra to watch violent or pornographic programmes not available on other TV channels they should be allowed to do so	61	*45*	67
I would find it easy to live without TV	42	37	41
Things that are likely to upset people should never be shown on television	38	**61**	**65**
I often switch from channel to channel and try to follow more than one programme at a time	25	**38**	**55**

As we have seen, viewers from minority groups expressed concern over the lack of positive role models on television, the continued use of stereotypical images and the effect of the medium on the young. Although white critics point to the on-screen presence of a number of blacks and Asians and see such a presence as positive, minority viewers see the issue as far more complex:

> ... when I look at Trevor MacDonald I just see a newsreader ... I don't see him as *Black* ... his mannerisms and voice are English.

In respect of popular drama many viewers lamented the fact that minorities were regularly and almost exclusively cast in demeaning roles like 'waiters in restaurants, but not barristers, lawyers or engineers'. In terms of newsreading and other presentational roles it was generally agreed that when a minority presenter did reach the screen the impact was often lost:

> If you look at Gargy Patel who reads the news ... when she
> started she was very Asian and as time goes on she becomes
> Westernised ... She's changed her make-up and clothes.

However not all minority viewers were quite so critical of such presenters:

> At least the Trevor MacDonalds, the Gargy Patels are *there* ...
> Some Asian woman can say 'that's a job I can do, I can be a
> newsreader', not just a sales assistant at Sainsbury's ...

But time and time again the sensitive issue of mixed marriages and the message such liaisons indicated were raised in discussion groups. The figure of Lenny Henry loomed large in discussions among both minority samples:

> He's racist ... his joke - Asians are all tech[nical] people, they
> own the whole of Russell Square where there are all those
> tellys, radios and all that on sale ... 'They worship Shiva and
> own Toshiba' ... that hurts me. He's no role model because of
> marrying a white spouse. It's giving the wrong picture, it's the
> old-fashioned idea of going up the social ladder by marrying a
> white person.

Table 52 represents summary findings to questions specifically concerning 'ethnic issues'. The results are again predictable. Compared to the main white sample the viewers from the Asian and African-Caribbean samples desired more freedom to express their values and cultures, believed that they should be given more access by television, and still believed that negative stereotypes about their culture continued to be portrayed on television. (88 per cent of the African-Caribbean sample and 76 per cent of the Asian sample believed that 'all too often TV portrays negative stereotypes' of minorities, compared to only 52 per cent of the main sample.) They also believed that it would be a good idea for ethnic minorities to have their own channels, although they did not necessarily believe that cable or satellite services offered more potential to establish such channels. All three samples of viewers strongly believed that 'programmes about particular ethnic minorities should be made by people from those communities'.

Table 52. Attitudes to ethnic issues - Summary

	Main Sample %	Asian Sample %	African Caribbean Sample %
This is a free country and people should be able to promote their ethnic values and cultures if they wish to	77	**91**	**90**
Programmes about particular ethnic minorities should be made by people from those communities	71	70	87
Television has a responsibility to allow access to ethnic minority groups	71	**86**	**88**
Television should cater for all the different ethnic communities found in Britain today	70	**89**	**90**
Comedy on television should not poke fun at ethnic minorities	66	**81**	**84**
Ethnic minority issues ought to be part of the regular television news coverage	63	**80**	**86**
Having a channel for a particular ethnic minority's programmes is a good idea	63	**75**	**78**
All too often TV portrays negative stereotypes about different ethnic minority groups	52	**76**	**88**
Cable or Satellite channels offer better opportunities than the mainstream channels for ethnic minorities to make their own programmes	46	50	50

Minority communities felt neglected by mainstream television programming and also were concerned about the effect of the medium on the young and impressionable:

> I'm concerned why our young black people have become so
> overtly aggressive ... in a lot of the youth they have low self-
> esteem ... imagery of blacks that is shown is often the
> American aggression, the American nastiness ... British TV
> doesn't do enough to say, look at the British people *here* - how
> many programmes talk about the hundreds and thousands of
> blacks who are going to be over 65 over the next year and who
> have no intention of going back to the Caribbean?

It is perhaps impossible accurately to assess the hurt and injury felt by such
minorities at the negative stereotypical images they continue to see regularly
on the small screen. For example an Asian viewer expressed her personal
sense of injustice and of being profoundly misunderstood:

> We don't have a sense of humour. We're just these serious
> people who have just come over. I mean we're *not* like the
> first generation who came over ... in dramas and soap operas
> it's always the same scenario - an Asian woman is suppressed
> by the whole family, she doesn't have a mind of her own, all
> she ever does is what her husband tells her to do ... it is wrong
> ... a lot of Asian women are perfectly happy with their lives in
> this country yet they're never shown in that way.

Many Asian viewers specifically mentioned *My Beautiful Launderette* and *The
Buddha of Suburbia* as being particularly offensive representations of their
culture. But it was the generic themes of the negative stereotypes that were
considered to be especially damaging. For example a number of Asian viewers
expressed objection to one traditional stereotype:

> The humble ... you know ... the submissive Asian woman who
> doesn't have a mind of her own ... 'Oh sahib', you know the
> humble one who does anything to please ... yes sir, no sir,
> three bags full sir ... unfortunately some of our older
> generation believe that - they think we should be grateful we're
> in this country, when it's ours by right. You came over there
> and nicked everything from us, at least we have the decency to
> work for what we want ...

Most minority viewers - from both the Asian and African-Caribbean samples - were pessimistic, and felt that nothing would be done to rectify negative stereotyping. For example no one particularly expressed a belief in 'integrated casting' as a solution:

> To say that you can find a black-skinned man who could go out on the TV as just a character is very difficult, cos they'll always look at the face. He won't always have a straight nose, he'll often have a broader nose ...

Within the two minority samples Asian viewers expressed the opinion that even the black minorities were better treated than they were. One Asian viewer believed that, despite the problem both cultures shared in being misrepresented, there were more positive American programmes black people could respond to:

> We're both in the same boat, but there's some programmes that portray them properly like *The Cosby Show* or *The Fresh Prince of Bel Air* ... although there are others like *Desmond's* which do show them in a negative way. But at least there is some *balance*, whereas on the whole every time I see an Asian on television I am offended.

Both Asian and African-Caribbean viewers believed that the colonial mentality was still present - perhaps unconsciously or at least unintentionally - and that behind the negative stereotyping of their cultures on television lay a sense of white superiority:

> The attitude is 'this is a Western culture, this is the best culture', everything else is alien. They don't really try to understand the black culture at all.

An Asian viewer expressed a commonly-held fear that their own culture was under constant threat of emasculation by the dominant white culture:

> Asian youngsters are forgetting their languages, their culture ... this white society wants them just to assimilate to forget their culture.

What most concerned the majority of viewers from both minority samples was not only the way in which racist stereotypes pandered to white racists and reduced the self-esteem of Asian and African-Caribbean people, but also its quite divisive consequences:

> I remember I used to dread watching it [*Till Death Us Do Part*] because I hated going to school the day after, I hated it, and I hated documentaries on India because I didn't want to be ridiculed ... Alf Garnett taught them a whole new language of what to call us ... but my brother loved it ... the racism seeps into our own community and the people don't even realise it.

Part Three

The Future of Television and Ethnic Relations

6 ALTERNATIVE TELEVISION

Despite the existence of such programmes as *African Express*, *Black Bag*, *East*, *Funky Black Shorts* and other 'minority programmes', the 1994 survey unequivocally demonstrated that ethnic minorities from both the Asian and African-Caribbean communities are far from happy with what they see on contemporary television. From their point of view it tends to stereotype them and present negative images of their culture, with an unnecessary and unjust over-emphasis on the one hand on black criminality and on the other hand on images of Asian people as mere victims. In the crucial area of popular prime-time television fiction there are few positive characters from either community regularly visible on the screen and overall, on fictional (and indeed factual) television, there is a distinct lack of balance - they believe. Minority viewers might well tolerate a number of stories, say, about Yardies, black-on-black violence and crack-cocaine if such stories were counterbalanced by more positive and life-enhancing narratives. Karen Ross succinctly summarises the overall situation concerning the representation of ethnic minorities within popular fictional television when she argues that:

> The lack of black and Asian characters in popular television would not be so significant - the frequency of black and Asian appearances is roughly in proportion to their number in the population generally - if such roles displayed the full diversity of human experience in everyday life. This is not, however, the case. Where are the strong, positive, leading roles for ethnic minority artists? Where are the black women challenging traditional male attitudes? Where are the young Asian people surviving the rigours of adolescence in ordinary households? It is the enactment of normal, ordinary, everyday life which is fundamentally missing from popular television fictions, where actors are allowed to act outside their skin rather than in constant reference to it.[1]

Minority viewers determinedly believe that such negative stereotyping together with lack of balance only reinforce prejudice, or indeed help create it in the first place. There is, in addition, the concern expressed by the older generation that the ethnic identities of the Asian and African-Caribbean young are under constant threat through the continual perpetuation of the supremacy of white culture. There is, to a degree, a sense of resignation over television's performance and in these matters they see little prospect of change. Reluctantly, it must be added, such viewers tentatively believe that the niche cable and satellite channels may potentially act more in line with their interests and be supportive to their cultures.

Other Ethnic Minorities

It is of course not only Asian and African-Caribbean viewers who complain about ethnic stereotyping and misrepresentation. For example Irish viewers complain both of stereotyping and of the removal from the screen of such programming as Gaelic football which speaks to their culture. Similarly members of the Greek Cypriot community[2] have consistently complained of the stereotyping of their culture in such programmes as *Birds of a Feather* and of Cypriot individuals as in Harry Enfield's character Stavros. One episode of *Birds of a Feather*, for example, included the funeral of the mother of 'Chris', the programme's British Cypriot cockney. Rather than representing a realistic image of such mourning, Cypriot actor Peter Polycarpou (as Chris) and the other Cypriot actors/extras were seen drunk, sexually molesting the female mourners by pinching their bottoms, and by dancing the Zorba. In another episode which greatly upset such viewers, Pauline Quirke's character, Sharon, remarked that of course she couldn't possibly be perceived as 'a Greek wife, as I ain't got a moustache'. One reader of the Greek Cypriot newspaper *Parikiaki* was so enraged that she wrote to say that in her opinion the BBC obviously saw Cypriots as a 'soft target', and that they wouldn't dream of attacking another ethnic minority's so called *characteristics*: 'I can't be an African wife, I aven't got thick lips'.[3]

Overall *Birds of a Feather* tended to portray Cypriots as being somewhat insular and unfriendly people with Mafia-type leanings, and Greek Cypriot women specifically as drab, scarf-wearing and occasionally moustached. It is surely fair to argue that, as the Cypriot community already suffers from under-representation on television, such images can only serve to perpetuate certain stereotypes that may already be held by some members of the British viewing public. The only character on popular television considered to be an accurate (and more-rounded) representation of the Cypriot personality and

90

culture is 'Nick Georgiadis', a fireman from *London's Burning*. From the more distant past Kojak, too, is remembered with a degree of affection.

In reality the British Greek Cypriot home entertainment system is characterised by a number of television sets, together with multiple decoders. The older Greek Cypriots - 1950s first generation immigrants - watch both Greek and Cypriot State television beamed in by satellite, while their children may watch the main broadcast channels. The grandchildren might well tune into Sky. Many Greek Cypriot viewers express a hope that Hellenic Television (and other British-based Greek cable stations) will concentrate on the teaching of Greek and also provide additional 'local' community programming.

Despite there being an estimated 300,000 Jews living in Britain, they, like other minorities, suffer constant stereotyping and misrepresentation on mainstream television:

> If your contact with Jews was through television, you would think we were obsessed - with the Holocaust, with Israel, with our nails, with Rabbis, with the strictly orthodox in Stamford Hill... Jewish characters and issues thinly dot the schedules on the four main channels as well as the satellite stations but paint an incomplete and often inaccurate picture of the reality of Anglo-Jewish life.[4]

On recent British popular television there are few Jewish characters who have appeared on a regular basis: most notably there was Jane Lapotaire as the rabbi in *Love Hurts*, Sam Saturday the Jewish detective (in the short-lived series of the same name), the central characters in *Every Silver Lining* and *So Haunt Me* and, memorably, actress Lesley Joseph as an Essex Jewish princess with deadly nails in the aforementioned *Birds of a Feather*.

Of course more memorably *The Rag Trade circa* 1961 was the first British television series not only to be set in a clothing factory, but also the first to feature Jews. It was later to be followed by such one-off programmes as the *Bar Mitzvah Boy* (1976) and series like *Never Mind the Quality, Feel the Width* (1967) and *So You Think You've Got Troubles* (1991).

On British television Jews indeed spend a lot of the time 'wallowing in the documentary ghetto',[5] but such programming is of course not as influential in the shaping of popular consciousness as drama, especially soaps. The 1993 one-off BBC drama, *Wall of Silence,* generally created uproar in the Jewish community because its story of the supposedly ritualistic murder of a local butcher for being a would-be *moiser* (or informer) was seen to present a wildly inaccurate picture of Chasidic Jews, and it was believed that it might incite anti-Semitism. In the soaps very few Jewish characters have emerged: *Coronation Street* featured bookmaker Benjamin Lewis in 1973-74; Elsa Feldman appeared in *Emmerdale* (1989), while *EastEnders* has featured four Jewish characters, most notably the somewhat elusive Dr Legg and the feisty sociology lecturer Rachel Kaminsky. *Brookside,* set in Liverpool - in actuality a city with a sizeable Jewish population - and avowedly a social-realist soap, has conversely failed to produce a single Jewish character: blacks, a Chinese family, a religious cult, lesbians, murderers, drug-dealers have all stalked the close, but there has been no room for Jewish characters.

By contrast Jewish characters feature regularly and quite substantively on American TV: one is the enthusiastic and emotionally-driven Dr Greene in Channel 4's *ER* who spends most of his time 'saving lives rather than suffering from Holocaust angst'.[6] But perhaps the most interesting Jewish character from American television, also on Channel 4, is *Northern Exposure*'s Dr Joel Fleischman, a New York physician reluctantly marooned in the outbacks of Cicely, Alaska. In one memorable episode he needed a *minyan* in order to recite *Kaddish* for his deceased Uncle Manny, so in keeping with their sense of camaraderie, the multi-cultural residents of Cicely were determined somehow to find him nine Jewish men.[*] None of the Jewish men that Joel's Cicely friends brought to him had anything in common with him, however, so in the final scene of the episode Joel was seen reciting *Kaddish* in Hebrew, surrounded by the familiar faces of his friends, having rejected the Jewish strangers.[7]

Multicultural Programming

The term 'multicultural programming' on television is almost as vague as the notion of a 'multicultural society'. It must centre on the idea of the respect for, and acceptance of, cultural diversity, but as John Rex has argued there are many individuals 'to whom the very idea of multi-culturalism is anathema' and who would 'oppose the emphasis upon diversity'.[8]

---

[*] In the Orthodox Jewish religion there has to be 10 Jewish men for a service to take place. *Kaddish* is the Jewish prayer for the dead (and women are not allowed to say it).

Within broadcasting itself there is, nevertheless, a great enthusiasm and advocacy for the idea of such multicultural programming:

> Multicultural programming ... by making cultural diversity part of the reality of television and radio it aims to shift the focus of the listener and viewer away from the conflict model of us and them. For example, drama series set in the country should show its diversity. Quiz shows should represent the mix of contestants, the diverse make-up of society. News and Current Affairs should not merely focus on the problems represented by black/migrant communities but see them as part of ongoing reality.[9]

It is believed that such programming would have a 'profound effect on the perceptions and attitudes of the viewing and listening public', and that it would undoubtedly challenge 'racist ideas'.[10] Clearly the respondents of the 1994 survey were less enthusiastic: they neither felt that they were in fact watching multicultural broadcasting, nor did they feel they were likely to do so in the foreseeable future.

One of the avowed principles of multicultural broadcasting is that it must at one and the same time be both 'broadcast' *and* 'narrowcast': 'there can be no ghetto, yet there must be programmes that cater for sub-sectors'.[11] Such a dual aim has inevitably led to complexity and also controversy. It was a much easier task in earlier decades, like the 1960s, when, for example, the BBC produced items for the newly-arriving immigrants from Asia. Such programmes as *Make Yourself At Home* and *New Life* were minor and quite subtle attempts at social engineering. More recently the BBC has decided that its Asian programming should be voiced in English, ostensibly aimed at the newer and younger generation, and, additionally, in order for it to be 'accessible to the widest possible audience'.[12] Channel 4 too is unashamed to assert that they have to 'get the ratings' for their multicultural programmes and thus proudly report that 'there are five times as many non-West Indians watching [*Desmond's*] as there are West Indians'.[13] But clearly such a philosophy is not particularly shared by viewers from ethnic minorities. Generally speaking they see television (especially terrestrial television) as white television, and consequently seek out individual programmes which are black and Asian and, in the case of the latter minority, are programmes broadcast in indigenous Asian languages. That is what *they* actually mean by multicultural programming.

Affirmative Action

The Commission for Racial Equality believes that, with the removal of discriminatory practices, the talent and ability of ethnic minorities will be translated into actual employment opportunities. Others are less optimistic. A number of black activists, for example, are more enthusiastic about the alternative strategy of positive discrimination and embrace the contemporary American notion of affirmative action. Indeed the BBC itself has for a number of years formally set targets of employing at least 8 per cent of its staff from ethnic minorities. But, as Salim Salam points out, despite the fact that such a target has been exceeded each year 'most of those staff are security personnel, cleaners or other manual grade workers, not involved in production at all'. Salam laments the fact that there 'are hardly any black people at Producer and Senior Producer levels' and 'even fewer heads of department or other senior executives'.[14]

An added problem, and one we have already noted in Chapter 1, is that of the marginalisation of the interests, priorities and skills of minorities despite the slight increase of recruitment into mainstream television: 'aspiring drama writers are sent to black comedy, game show directors told to apply to *The Real McCoy*, the potential *Panorama* producer to *All Black* or *East*'.[15] Some black and Asian producers understandably do not wish to be saddled with such so-called 'ghetto programming' or indeed the 'burden of representation' that invariably accompanies such employment. Lenny Henry speaks for many black media professionals when he asks, 'why can't a black director direct *Jeeves and Wooster* or *Taggart*?' As he remarks, the scenario is not simply 'all oppression and tribulation. What about historical stories and musicals?'[16]

But whether black or Asian producers work in mainstream television, or in the 'ghetto slots',[17] it is often argued that their own values will invariably be subordinated to the more widespread media ones of the importance of high ratings, the power of sensationalism and the formats of tabloid television. Consider for instance the examples of BBC 2's *All Black* and *East*, two series which at times pander as much to the values of tabloid television as they do to the reality, interests and values of black and Asian cultures.

Satellite and Cable

In their 1989 submission to Government following the White Paper on Broadcasting, the Indian and Bangladeshi Workers Association claimed that

94

they not only wished to see more on-screen positive images of minorities but also recommended the introduction of a 'national channel that has only black programmes made by black programme makers'.[18] Interestingly enough when some time later ITC researchers asked minorities whether they wished to see special separate satellite or cable channels created for ethnic minorities, there was little enthusiasm for the idea.[19] By 1994, however, there was far more enthusiasm for such niche channels as the ITC Survey demonstrated, perhaps an indication of the growing pessimism as to the ability of mainstream terrestrial channels to change their programming.

It is an open question whether or not black or Asian sensibilities are best served by satellite and cable channels rather than terrestrial ones. Kobena Mercer rightly argues that while a future system of more deregulated television *may* bring more opportunities for minorities, it could be that 'under the pressure to be popular, a non-regulated media will inevitably squeeze out specialist or minority tastes and push black representation firmly back into the ghetto again'.[20] Some commentators, on the other hand, are concerned that if niche satellite and cable channels are enthusiastically subscribed to by minority audiences 'public service' broadcasting will simply relinquish its role in providing multicultural programming in any shape or form. As Frachon and Vargaftig observe, with a total of some 13 million people of 'foreign origin' living in Europe such a population represents a lucrative potential audience for niche 'ethnic channels'. The high production and start-up costs invariably mean that such channels operate by recycling old material or constantly repeating newer programmes. Despite such repetitive or less than original programming (and occasional material of poor quality) for many minority viewers such channels nonetheless may provide the only way that they see their culture reflected in broadcasting. There are however problems with such a blanket service:

> These so-called ethnic channels - and especially those based in Britain - are fortunate in that huge stocks of films and programmes are available from Hong Kong and India. However, although these channels are popular with first generation immigrants eager to watch programmes in their own languages, subsequent generations do not necessarily share their enthusiasm.[21]

It is within this inter-generational context that the major British Asian satellite and cable channels attempt to meet the conflicting demands of all the generations of minority viewers. For example, Asianet which is available in more than 180,000 cable households attempts to reduce the reliance on repeat programming to broadcast more 'first run' movies, and, most importantly, to develop 'local' programming. Zee TV (previously, TV Asia), on the other hand, is available in fewer than 25,000 cable households. Thus like Asianet much of its output consists of the recycling of Pakistani dramas and Indian films: *Tara,* a 135 episode serial, is described as 'revolving around four friends who studied in college together. Four close friends yet each with different characters. We witness the path their lives follow, and how they intertwine. A host of other characters prop up the story'. Zee TV also broadcasts numerous game shows and quizzes, such as *Film Deewane* and *Saanp Seedi* (or *Snakes and Ladders)*, as well as programmes for women, fashion magazine programmes, children's items and talk shows like *Chakravyuh*. In this latter show 'controversial' items such as 'should minors work?', 'should doctors be accountable?' are discussed by one of India's most well-known celebrities, Vinod Dua:

> Watch him gently ease information, views, opinions on a spectrum of issues where tact and discretion give way to open-hearted, no holds barred discussions. *Chakravyuh* is one of the very first talk shows in India that has raised issues that were previously taboo. Stimulating, novel, riveting you never know what issue will come next on Zee TV's programme...'

Identity Television, a major British black cable channel, is available in more than 220,000 UK households. It broadcasts for some 18 hours a day in 3 x 6 hour sequences. Over half of its output is music - ranging from soul rap, hip-hop, jungle, reggae, ragga, gospel, soca and calypso - although the channel also broadcasts some comedy, soap, a number of dramas and a very small amount of current affairs programming. Older viewers tune in for the soaps, Caribbean material and religion, in contrast to the younger generation who are attracted solely by the musical output. The major proportion of Identity's material emanates from the library of its original USA partner Black Entertainment TV (BET).[22] It is somewhat safe and undemanding material, as in *227*, a long-standing drama serial:

> *227* is an ageing apartment building with lively unforgettable characters dwelling in it. Take Sandra Clarke, starring as the sassy, single lady who women can't stop talking about and men can't keep their eyes off; or Mary Jenkins starring Marla

96

Gibbs, who firmly believes in standing up for her rights and speaking her mind. At *227* neighbours share everything, gossip problems, but most of all laughs.

Another significant operator in the burgeoning cable/satellite marketplace is the satellite channel MBC which, from its London base, broadcasts all of its programmes in Arabic, primarily for the large potential audience in the Gulf (and secondarily for Muslim communities in Europe). The channel is funded at source by 'Saudi Arabian interests' and exchanges programming with a number of national broadcasters including Tunisia, Morocco, Kuwait, Djibouti, Algeria and Saudia Arabia. Programming includes (from Spain and Mexico) Arabic 'soap operas', Indian films (sub-titled or dubbed), sport, children's items, pop videos, fashion and other magazine-type programmes like *Bassat Al Rih* (*The Flying Carpet*). Broadcasts always start with a reading from the Holy Koran, while on Fridays Holy prayers are beamed live from Mecca. It is the news bulletins however which constitute the central and most significant items of the schedule. In the Gulf, for example, viewers will receive from MBC news which is not channelled through their own Ministry of Information. In practice MBC purchases the 'Reuters feed' but voices it according to its own interests. The news bulletins themselves exhibit quite different priorities, emphases and running-orders from the mainstream channels of the BBC, ITV and Channel 4. MBC's own promotional material emphasises the uniqueness - as it sees it - of its news programming:

> For the first time in the history of Arab television, viewers can watch and listen to the religion's traditional 'enemies' or historic opponents expressing their views and giving their own analysis on the same news bulletin ... never before had an Arab television viewer seen Palestinian and Israeli officials, stone throwing children, angry armed Jewish settlers and confused Israeli conscripts speaking directly to them all in one news item.

Such bulletins may well become of increasing interest (and concern) to regulators as well as to such alleged 'traditional *enemies*' as Israel. The European viewers of MBC - found in England, Holland, Denmark and Sweden to name just four countries - are Arabs who still wish to maintain their Arab identities..

The London-based Chinese Channel is yet another niche channel which has steadily increased its audiences with, in 1995, at least 20,000 Chinese

97

households being reached. It broadcasts from midnight to 7.00 am (due to satellite time restrictions), and the programming consists of same-day news from Hong Kong, movies from China, Hong Kong and Taiwan, drama and children's programmes. Not surprisingly its viewers heavily time-shift the channel. Almost three-quarters of the channel's material is purchased from TVB Hong Kong.

It is unlikely that in the future there will be any dramatic change to these current trends, and minority television will therefore increasingly be represented by cable and satellite niche channels, rather than by terrestrial television. It is an understatement to say that the political effect of such a 'separate existence on TV has yet to be seen'.[23] It is evident however that the notion of television as some kind of 'integrating' medium is anachronistic, and that no one could expect it to operate in such away in the late 1990s and beyond.

Agendas in Search of a Plot

Popular terrestrial television programming is perceived by those minority viewers questioned in the survey to be white television. Affirmative action along the lines of 'integrated casting' in popular drama for example is not generally seen as a strategy likely to succeed. In its simplest form the term means 'the acceptance of actors on the basis of ability rather than race',[24] unlike the conventions in which white actors 'black up' as Othello or Gandhi. Moreover, a black actor is unlikely to be cast as Tory politician Alan Clarke in the dramatisation of his diaries. But despite the enthusiasm for integrated casting of Anwar and Shang in the 1982 CRE Report - 'integrated casting on television would help to ease racial tension and promote mutual respect and understanding'[25] - it is unlikely to be widespread enough to succeed.

In an article on film-maker Woody Allen, Stuart Jeffries laments the fact that in Allen's 1995 movie *Bullets Over Broadway* he casts a 'stereotypical fat, black talking black maid, straight from central casting *circa* 1935'. He asks of Allen the question, 'isn't it shameful that a director who works almost exclusively in a city with a large black population has so few roles for black people in his movies?' Allen's response to the question was that he didn't think that affirmative action extended to people in movies:

> If I was doing a movie about a black jazz musician I would
> cast a black actor. But I don't have many black actors because

I write about what I know about. I don't know the nuances of black families. Spike Lee can do that and catch every gesture. I never think about it.[26]

Neither is affirmative action in the forum of 'quotas' likely to work, as witnessed in Isaac Julien's somewhat misconceived *Young Soul Rebels* (1991). Simply putting black actors on the screen may well be politically advantageous in the short-term, but without the accompaniment of interesting narratives and high production values, the victory is somewhat hollow.

It is difficult to avoid the conclusion that the Asian, black and other minority cultures have increasingly come to define themselves in opposition to white culture. Perhaps in future minority cultures will further develop their voice on separate channels and indeed separate media.

Notes

1   Ross (1992) p 29

2   Below is the ethnic classification used by the 1991 Census. Significantly for Greek and Turkish Cypriot communities they are subsumed under the generic heading of 'white'.

4-fold classification	10-fold classification	Full listing
White	White	White Irish Greek/Greek Cypriot Turkish/Turkish Cypriot Mixed White
Black groups	Black Caribbean	Black - Caribbean Caribbean Island West Indies Guyana
	Black African	Black - African Africa south of the Sahara
	Black other	Black - other

99

		Black - British
		Black - Mixed Black/White
		Black - Mixed Other
Indian/Pakistani/ Bangladeshi	**Indian**	Indian
	Pakistani	Pakistani
	Bangladeshi	Bangladeshi
Chinese and Others	**Chinese**	Chinese
	Other - Asian	East African Asian
		Indo-Caribbean
		Black-Indian sub-continent
		Black-other Asian
	Other - other	North Africa/Arab/Iranian
		Mixed Asian/White
		British ethnic minority (other)
		British (no indication)
		Other Mixed Black/White
		Other Mixed Asian/White
		Other Mixed - Other

From Owen (1992) p 14

3   *Parikiaki*, 31 March 1994

4   Victoria Stagg Elliot, 'Prime Time and Passed Over', *New Moon*, April 1995, pp 10-12

5   *Ibid* p 10

6   *Ibid* p 11

7   Helen Jacobus in the *Jewish Chronicle*, August 12, 1994

8   Rex (1985), p 16. See also David Theo Goldberg (1994a: 11), 'The emergence of contemporary multiculturalisms, then, is to be understood in relation to the twentieth-century dominance of monoculturalism'

9   Singh (1995) pp 65-66

100

10   *Ibid* p 66

11   Andy Fry, 'Out of the Ghetto,' *Broadcast*, 7 October 1994

12   Narendhra Morar of the BBC Multicultural Unit, quoted in Fry, *Ibid*

13   Farrukh Dhondy of Channel 4, quoted in Fry, *ibid.*

14   Salam (1995), p 69. See also Husband (1994a).

15   Phillips (1995), p 18

16   Quoted in Black *Film Bulletin*, Summer 1994, pp 14-16

17   See Philips (1995: 18) ' ... Whatever the shortcomings of the 'specialist' strategy it is true that many young programme makers who would not otherwise have made any productions had the opportunity to learn their craft on the so-called "ghetto" shows. The way to solve the diversion of talent is not to get rid of the only proven access for minority talent - it is to make sure that the other routes open up... '

18   Indian and Bangladeshi Workers Association (1989), p 7

19   Gunter, Fazal and Wober (1991), p 11

20   Mercer (1989), p 10

21   Frachon and Vargaftig (1995a), p 8

22   BET was bought in 1994 by HBO. Phillips (1995: 20) explains the acquisition as follows: ' ... HBO saw the need to colonize minority viewing early when they bought up the loss-making Black Entertainment TV organization. What HBO grasped was that minorities, partly because of low incomes and unemployment, tend to have disproportionately high levels of TV viewing. For a movie-based channel, such an audience is extraordinarily valuable, and any marginal marketing advantage - such as a black channel - would repay the marginal cost. HBO clearly believe that the same applies in the UK ... '

23   Phillips, *ibid* p 20

24   Anwar and Shang (1982), p 55

25   *Ibid* p 56. See also Ross (1992: 33) in which she describes the so-called superior integrated casting of *Brookside*'s Mike Johnson as compared with the ill-fated 'Chinese family'. Her argument fails to convince.

26.   Quoted in Stuart Jeffries 'King of Comedy', *The Guardian* April 10, 1995 Section II pp 2-3, 9

BIBLIOGRAPHY

Abdallah, Mogniss H (1995), 'Networking for migrant perspectives on television in France and Europe', pp 46-59, in Frachon and Vargaftig eds (1995).

Anwar, Muhammad and Shang, Anthony (1982), *Television in a Multi-Racial Society*, CRE: London.

Bourdon, Jérôme (1995), 'Foreigners on prime time or is television xenophobic?', pp 22-34, in Frachon and Vargaftig eds (1995).

Bourne, Stephen (1989), 'Introduction', pp 119-129, in Daniels and Gerson eds (1989).

Daniels, Therese and Gerson, Jane eds (1989), *The Colour Black*, BFI Publishing: London.

Dines, Gail and Humez, Jean M eds (1995), *Gender, Race and Class in Media*, Sage: London.

Drummond, Phillip, Paterson, Richard and Willis, Janet eds (1993), *National Identity and Europe*, BFI: London.

Frachon, Claire, and Vargaftig, Marion eds (1995), *European Television: Immigrants and Ethnic Minorities*, John Libbey: London.

Frachon, Claire and Vergaftig, Marion (1995a), 'Introduction', pp 3-9, in Frachon and Vargaftig eds (1995).

Fry, Andy (1994), 'Out of the Ghetto', *Broadcast*, October 7, p 34.

Fryer, Peter (1984), *Staying Power*, Pluto Press: London.

Gillespie, Marie (1993), 'Soap Viewing, Gossip and Rumour Amongst Punjabi Youth in Southall', pp 25-42, in Drummond *et al* eds (1993).

Goldberg, David Theo ed (1994), *Multiculturalism: A Critical Reader*, Basil Blackwell: Oxford.

Goldberg, David Theo (1994a), 'Introduction: Multicultural Conditions', pp 1-44, in Goldberg ed (1994).

Gray, Herman (1994), 'Television, Black Americans, and the American Dream', pp 176-187, in Newcomb, Horace ed (1994).

Gunter, Barrie, Fazal, Shehina, and Wober, Mallory (1991), *Ethnic Minority Attitudes to Broadcasting Issues*, ITC: London.

Hall, Stuart (1995), 'The Whites of Their Eyes: Racist Ideologies and the Media', pp 18-22, in Dines and Humez eds (1995)

Hamamoto, Darrell Y (1994), *Monitored Peril*, University of Minnesota Press: Minneapolis.

Hartman, Paul and Husband, Charles (1974), *Racism and the Mass Media*, Davis-Poynter: London.

Henry, Lenny (1994), 'Dramatic licence', *Black Film Bulletin*, Summer, pp 15-16.

Husband, Charles ed (1994), *A Richer Vision*, UNESCO/John Libbey: Paris/London.

Husband, Charles (1994a), 'General Introduction: ethnicity and media democratization within the nation-state', pp 1-19, in Husband ed (1994).

Husband, Charles (1994b), 'Conclusion', pp 143-145, in Husband ed (1994).

Hussein, Ali (1994), 'Market forces and the marginalization of Black film and video production in the United Kingdom', pp 127-142, in Husband ed (1994).

Indian Workers/Bangladeshi workers (1989), *Racism in Broadcasting*, Birmingham.

Kingsley, Hilary, and Tibballs, Geoff (1989), *Box of Delights*, Macmillan: London.

Medhurst, Andy (1989), 'Introduction', pp 15-21, in Daniels and Gerson eds (1989).

Mercer, Kobena (1989), 'General Introduction', pp 1-12, in Daniels and Gerson eds (1989).

Myant, Chris (1995), 'Television and racial equality: How the Race Relations Act has helped', pp 35-44, in Frachon and Vargaftig eds (1995).

Newcomb, Horace ed (1994), *Television: The Critical View*, Oxford University Press: New York.

Owen, David (1992), *Ethnic Minorities in Great Britain: Settlement Patterns*, CRER: Warwick.

Owen, David (1993), *Ethnic Minorities in Great Britain: Age and Gender Structure*, CRER: Warwick.

Owen, David (1993a), *Ethnic Minorities in Great Britain: Economic Characteristics*, CRER: Warwick.

Owen, David (1993b), *Ethnic Minorities in Great Britain: Housing and Family Characteristics*, CRER: Warwick.

Owen, David (1993c), *Country of Birth: Settlement Patterns*, CRER: Warwick.

Owen, David (1994), *Black People in Great Britain: Social and Economic Circumstances*, CRER: Warwick.

Owen, David (1994a), *South Asian People in Great Britain: Social and Economic Circumstances*, CRER: Warwick.

Owen, David (1994b), *Chinese People and 'Other' Ethnic Minorities in Great Britain: Social and Economic Circumstances*, CRER: Warwick.

Paterson, Richard (1993), 'Collective Identity, Television and Europe', pp 1-

9, in Drummond et al eds (1993).

Perotti, Antonio (1995), 'The Council of Europe's guidelines 1992-1992', pp 76-87, in Frachon and Vargaftig eds (1995).

Phillips, Trevor (1995), 'UK TV: A place in the sun?, pp 13-21, in Frachon and Vargaftig eds (1995).

Pines, Jim (1989), 'Introduction', pp 63-70, in Daniels and Gerson eds (1989).

Rahi, Jag (1992), *Religious Broadcasting, Religious Minority Research*, Counterpoint Research/ITC: London.

Rex, John (1985), *The Concept of a Multi-cultural Society*, Occasional Papers in Ethnic Relations No 3, Centre for Research in Ethnic Relations: University of Warwick.

Ross, Karen (1992), *Television in Black and White*, RPER 19, Centre for Research in Ethnic Relations: University of Warwick.

Salam, Salim (1995), 'A mirror crack'd from side to side: Black independent producers and the television industry', pp 68-75, in Frachon and Vargaftig eds (1995).

Singh, Europe (1995), 'From Monochrome to Technicolour', pp 60-67, in Frachon and Vargaftig eds (1995).

Solomon, Frances-Anne (1994), 'Dramatic license', *Black Film Bulletin*, Summer, pp 14-16.

Stam, Robert and Shohat, Ella (1994), 'Contested Histories: Eurocentrism, Multiculturalism, and the Media', pp 296-324, in Goldberg ed (1994).

Wober, J M (1987), *TV and The Third World*, IBA:London.

Wober, J M and Fazal, S (1984), *Citizens of Ethnic Minorities, Their Prominence in Real Life and on Television*, IBA: London.